MAROON5

SHOOTING FOR THE STARS

MAROON5

SHOOTING FOR THE STARS

CHLOÉ GOVAN

OMNIBUS PRESS

London / New York / Paris / Sydney / Copenhagen / Berlin / Madrid / Tokyo

Cover designed by Fresh Lemon
Picture research by Jacqui Black

ISBN: 978.1.78035.043.7
Order No: OP55330

Exclusive Distributors
Music Sales Limited,
14/15 Berners Street,
London, W1T 3LJ.

Music Sales Corporation
180 Madison Avenue, 24th Floor,
New York,
NY 10010,
USA.

Macmillan Distribution Services,
56 Parkwest Drive
Derrimut, Vic 3030,
Australia.

Every effort has been made to trace the copyright holders of the photographs in this book but one or two were unreachable. We would be grateful if the photographers concerned would contact us.

Printed in the EU

A catalogue record for this book is available from the British Library.

Visit Omnibus Press on the web at www.omnibuspress.com

Contents

1

High Life In The City Of Showbiz

"**W**HICH Hollywood stereotype is more accurate?" quizzed one interviewer audaciously. "Everyone's gay or everyone's on cocaine?"

Adam Levine smiled wryly in the face of this archetypically forthright American line of interrogation, barely missing a beat before retorting, with equally good humour, "Both. Everyone's gay and everyone's on cocaine." He was talking about his hometown of Brentwood, the suburb of Los Angeles that had given birth to Maroon 5.

(In contrast, its British namesake, in the county of Essex, is home to no one more noteworthy than the cast of reality show *The Only Way Is Essex* – a national laughing stock for their excessive application of neon-orange fake tan.)

Brentwood, USA, boasted a prolific number of A-listers crammed into one zip code – and, courtesy of the world-famous Californian climate, none of them needed to top up their naturally sun-kissed glows. Representing the film world, there was Ben Affleck, Reese Witherspoon, Gwyneth Paltrow, Josh Duhamel and his wife, Fergie of the Black Eyed Peas. Then of course there was the iconic Marilyn Monroe, who had lived and died in Brentwood, and Nicole Brown-Simpson, whose gory murder made headlines after she and her friend Ron Goldman were found stabbed to death outside her condo on Bundy Drive. Her ex-husband, OJ Simpson, was charged with her murder but acquitted in a criminal trial, thanks to a defence team that included his friend Robert Kardashian – a man whose children would, in the true spirit of LA, later become reality TV stars.

Yet another famous Brentwood resident was Arnold Schwarzenegger –

the actor, bodybuilder and politician latterly known to the celebrity gossip crowd for refusing a sniffling, borderline hysterical Paris Hilton's plea, in his capacity of Governor of California, to rescue her from an 'unjust' jail sentence for a driving offence. In LA County, even Paris, a walking man-magnet, could fail to charm her way out of trouble – perhaps due to the competition. Put simply, every other impeccably manicured girl in this upmarket suburb seemed equally irresistible; Gisele Bundchen, the world's best paid supermodel in her prime, had made millions while based in this corner of the city of dreams.

The world's most eminent actors, singers, models, businessmen and businesswomen – along with a heady mixture of socialites and professional partiers – all made Brentwood their home for good reason. It offered all the glamour of the showbiz industry and the fast-paced excitement of the city without the less desirable grit, poverty and gang warfare of downtown LA. It was also at a different latitude, offering a cool respite from the suffo-cating heat of a Californian summer's day. Its invigorating ocean breezes made locals feel as though they were on permanent vacation.

Even more irresistibly, the scent of obscene wealth wafted through the air, putting London's Knightsbridge or New York's Manhattan to shame – no zip code was better designed to impress. Eye-wateringly expensive condos saluted the skyline, with two bedrooms sometimes setting back their buyer over $5 million. Penthouse suites boasted gleaming marble floors, winding spiral staircases, full-length windows, huge open-air balco-nies, high-end art plastered across the walls and – the biggest selling point of all – unobstructed ocean views. From this vantage point, only sea separated the hilltop homeowner from a mass of glittering skyscrapers in the city below. Fortunes were made and lost there, but Brentwood was a welcome retreat from that world – a lush, green, palm-studded oasis of calm. As Adam Levine would proudly enquire, why would any West Coast resident want to be elsewhere?

Adam's uncle, TV producer and writer Peter Noah, was one of those who'd long ago succumbed to Brentwood's charms. Perhaps conspicuous success had been hard-wired into the family's DNA, as the highlight of Peter's career was a senior production role on political drama *The West Wing*, winner of 29 industry awards. Audaciously set in the White House, it was famed for its daringly pointed fictional portrayal of real-life political controversies – as such, it was a political statement in itself. Parodying events such as homophobia scandals, terrorism, relations with the Middle East and the infamous Monica Lewinsky affair that shamed Bill Clinton, one of the show's biggest successes was its ability to pack a political punch whilst simultaneously dodging the censors.

Meanwhile, Peter's brother, Timothy Noah, broke into a similarly creative career as a journalist and author. Basing himself in Washington, the USA's political heart, he became an activist for the poor and dis-possessed while writing for *The Wall Street Journal, New York Times, Wash-ington Post, Slate* and *New Republic,* to name but a few. He also penned *The Great Divergence: America's Growing Inequality Crisis And What We Can Do About It,* in which he raged that the top one per cent of earners in the USA collected almost 20 per cent of the nation's income. A passionate Demo-crat, he argued that university tuition fees were spiralling out of control in a sorely unregulated market, depriving some talented students of a first-class education. He criticised Americans for their tendency to buy cut-price goods produced overseas, benefiting China and India while the home production market haemorrhaged jobs. The nation's immigration policy also went under the microscope, as he challenged the influx of low-skilled migrants and the competition it created for low-paid jobs. Timothy also advocated higher taxes for the wealthy, an increase in the minimum wage and a greater role for labour unions, his socialist leanings presenting a stark contrast to his privileged upbringing. His views also naturally invited some opposition; while all well-meaning citizens agreed that poverty was an unwanted burden, they were sharply divided as to causes and cures. The arguments raged on, but Timothy knew he had a definite ally in fellow current affairs journalist Marjorie Williams – the woman he'd first met at Harvard University, who became his wife.

Together, she and Timothy were A-list voyeurs of high-powered politics, discreetly scribbling their observations into notepads to be unveiled in the media later. Their line of work offered a sought-after pass into the world of US politics, with all its adrenalin-fuelled drama and subterfuge. Marjorie's best-selling memoirs, *The Woman At The Washington Zoo,* gave the inside stories of "Barbara Bush's stepmother quaking with fear at the mere thought of angering the First Lady and of Bill Clinton angrily telling Al Gore why he failed to win the presidency".

9

With a brother and sister-in-law who profiled the political elite for a living, rubbing shoulders with the President's family, and another brother's award-winning work on national television, Patsy Noah's life seemed positively tame in comparison. She ambled through life as an admissions counsellor, coaching teenagers on which university course would best suit their needs – it was fulfilling, but far from scintillating. She felt she had a job rather than a career, working to live instead of living to work. Consequently, when she met and married wealthy lawyer Fred Levine – a Berkeley graduate like herself – she wholeheartedly threw herself into her new role as wife and mother.

The first child to arrive was Adam, born on March 18, 1979. He would be closely followed by a brother, Michael. Mere months after Adam was born, his father had a change of career inspired by the high-fashion clothing companies he represented as a lawyer. He decided, together with his style-conscious sister Mardi, to set up his own fashion house; thus M. Frederic was conceived and, via Mardi's experience as a fashion buyer, the siblings created a wholesale list of designer couture and obscure boutique brands to sell in-store. The project quickly took off and, by the time Adam was ready to enrol in primary education, Fred could afford to send him to the prestigious, fee-paying Brentwood School.

The fees were eye-wateringly high at $27,000 a year for prep school alone, but Fred had ambitions for his son. There were three exclusive universities nearby – UCLA, Stanford and Berkeley – and their exacting standards made them difficult to gain entry to. All the same, a degree from any of them would almost guarantee a job in any field upon graduation. Little did he know how far his son would veer off that prescribed path; in fact, according to Adam himself, he would "never do any work".

But his infatuation with music was evident from an early age. "As a child, he would dance around in front of the mirror with a karaoke machine," chuckled one anonymous school friend to the author. "Actually, everyone thought he was gay!"

The soundtrack to his pop-star posturing was the hugely popular Michael Jackson. "I remember *Thriller* was just everyone's soundtrack," Adam would tell *ABC News* later. "It was the biggest record on earth and everyone wanted to be Michael Jackson. I'd dance around the living room with my glove on [to be like him]!"

Even earlier, he fell in love with the 1982 single 'Electric Avenue' by Eddy Grant, which was inspired by riots in south London's notorious Brixton neighbourhood and took its name from a local market street. When it crossed over stateside, it made it to number two on the chart – and it would be the first vinyl Adam ever bought. "I made my parents listen to it all the time," he would later recall with a glint of mischief in his eye. "I probably drove them a little crazy, so I am sorry to my parents for that. My family is a very musical family, they appreciate music, but I was OBSESSED with this tune. I loved that song so much . . . it's irresistible!"

He was equally enamoured with Hall and Oates, a duo who reached their peak in the mid-eighties with a combination of soft rock and R&B. However, as he grew older Adam began to temper his musical obsessions with other pastimes. Brentwood School had an emphasis on sport, boasting an impressive number of Olympic medallists among its alumni – and an insatiably competitive Adam was out to win a trophy. With his father as a basketball coach, that moment came sooner than he'd imagined; aged just six, he led his team to victory at a YMCA championship game, making the winning shot a second before time was called. "It turned me into an optimist," he would recall of that moment, "and a cocky son of a bitch."

In a school full of young boys, excelling at sport created a status close to godliness. An increasingly popular Adam was befriended by Ryan Dusick who was two years his senior, an age gap seen as an eternity by his peers. He also topped up his cool credentials by forging a friendship with equally popular pupil (and future Hollywood actor) Jake Gyllenhaal, who had known Adam "since we were in diapers". However, the would-be sporting hero's lucky spell was short-lived; that same year, the world as he knew it would split right down the middle when his parents divorced.

In a strange confluence of jilted women, his mother would move in with her husband's brother's newly single ex-wife and her young daughter, whom Adam soon regarded as a sister. He would spend weekdays with the three females, while every weekend he would travel across town to be with his father.

The changes were disorientating yet inevitable, and a powerless Adam soon began to channel his frustrations into rock music. His first concert, aged 10, was the LA-based glam-metal group Warrant, whose angry, frenetic sound represented how he felt inside.

11

A more soothing experience was his first kiss, with a precocious 11-year-old named Katie. "She asked me to take a walk after dinner," Adam recalled. "We walked 10 feet west of the cafeteria, which felt like forever. She went in for the kiss. I was freaked out and amazed. Then it got weird, once I got comfortable and started experimenting."

In that same year, 1990, he reunited with his friend Ryan for a rendition of the Bob Dylan song 'Knockin' On Heaven's Door' (as transformed into a rock anthem by Guns N' Roses), which was recorded in the latter's garage. Ryan stumblingly played as much as he knew of the drum part, while Adam took vocals and guitar – and the encounter was the beginning of a renewed love affair with music.

"When I was in school, I was a little rebellious," he'd later tell *ABC News*. "I wanted to play music. I didn't want to do the things they were teaching me. I picked up a guitar and that was it. The second I picked up a guitar, I never really put it down again – I fell so madly in love with it, it's all I did. It consumed my every thought and I'd have friends over that didn't even play instruments and I would just put instruments in their hands."

During this time, despite strong Jewish traditions on both sides of the family, he shunned a bar mitzvah: the traditional coming-of-age ceremony that routinely took place for boys of his faith upon turning 13. "I didn't want to have a bar mitzvah because I didn't feel that it was honest," he told *Blender*. "A lot of kids around me were having bar mitzvahs to cash in and I thought, 'If I wanted to be good with God, I certainly wouldn't want to do that.' I didn't feel it was sincere. Plus I didn't want to learn all that Hebrew!" He later added disapprovingly, "Trying to make a bunch of money . . . I just don't think it's the most respectful way to deal with God and beliefs and years and years and years of cultural heritage."

Thus, while his peers were revelling in the praise and attention, and expensive gifts, Adam quietly bowed out. Although he identified with the spiritual side, neither he nor his parents were attached to organised religion – having already established an anti-authoritarian reputation at school, he was not one for following a rulebook.

In the years to come, in spite of the stern, dark warning issued in the Old Testament's Book Of Leviticus 19:28 ("You shall not make any tattoo marks on yourselves"), he went on to smother himself in body art, from an obligatory guitar motif to the ultimate religious no-no – a scantily clad pin-up girl.

In Adam's eyes, he flaunted the rules for a reason. He preferred to set his own moral compass quite apart from the rigid teachings of the Torah, with his main aim being never to intentionally hurt anyone. In any case, by this point he was reluctant to spend time on anything that would take his focus away from music.

Like a child on the loose in a candy store, he devoured as many musical genres as he could – from jazz and torch-song greats like Frank Sinatra, Ella Fitzgerald and Billie Holiday to classic pop-rock icons such as the Beatles and their Britpop descendants, Oasis. He even found time for guilty pleasures like the so-called frivolous bubblegum pop of the Cardigans.

However, his biggest influences by far were punk rock, grunge and heavy metal – and every combination thereof. Tapping into those trends throughout the nineties produced an edgy, at times even grungy sound; he became obsessed with Green Day, Pearl Jam, Nirvana, Fugazi and Weezer. He would listen to those bands' classics on repeat, striving to memorise the chords and expanding his own musical horizons to playing bass, piano and drums.

In fact, an overzealous Adam almost deafened himself in the process. "I learned how to play drums in my attic listening to 'Doctor Feelgood', the Mötley Crüe record," he later revealed to *ABC News*. "I had a karaoke machine that I'd put, it was a really bad idea, but I put it right by my ear in order to get it loud enough," he confessed. "I'd have to crank it all the way. I just had these drums, a really crappy drum set. I would be listening to it and playing it, almost treating it like a monitor and I'd have it rigged up so it was blasting in my face . . . and I learned how to play drums. So thank you, Tommy Lee, appreciate it!"

As his obsession grew, Adam cajoled his mother into footing the bill for a programme at the French Woods Festival of the Performing Arts Summer Camp – a seemingly innocuous decision that would change his life forever. Located in the Catskill Mountains – only two and a half hours from New York City but blissfully remote – the camp offered a retreat free from the distractions of modern living, for students to immerse themselves in music. Accommodation came in the form of Scandinavian-style wooden chalets where, back in those days, mobile phone signals were totally non-existent. The mountains formed a protective barricade against the outside world; for Adam, who would later be diagnosed with the condition ADHD, it provided a perfect setting for him to offset his growing problems with attention and focus.

Free from the distraction of creature comforts and technology, he concentrated on writing and producing songs at the camp's surprisingly state-of-the-art recording studio. As part of the programme, students were also encouraged to form their own bands; although Adam had briefly disappeared off the social radar, his networking at this unlikely highland hideaway would make life-changing connections. It was here that he bonded with fellow Brentwood School student and bandmate-to-be Jesse Carmichael – then a clarinet and guitar player who might easily have won a Separated At Birth contest for his resemblance to a young Paul McCartney.

Born on April 2, 1979, Jesse had started life in Boulder, Colorado, before moving to LA as an infant to follow his father's burgeoning career in the TV industry. Bob Carmichael made a name for himself as a director and cameraman on documentaries, commercials and full-length features, specialising in coverage of daredevil adventure sports. His footage focused on such sports as bungee-jumping and extreme skiing, and he filmed the first ever all-woman mountain climbing show to be televised in the USA. He also co-wrote a climbing-themed screenplay, *Fall Line*, which was produced in 1978, and worked with clients such as Adidas, Reebok and Burger King. The peak of his career would be winning an Emmy Award.

However, aside from a love of the films of legendary director Stanley Kubrick, Jesse's interests did not mirror his father's – his lay in music. Like Adam, his tape collection included the Cardigans, Radiohead, the Beatles, Supergrass and Fugazi – but he was also able to introduce his new friend to Blur, Pavement, Beck, Paul Weller, Elvis Costello, Elastica, Ocean Colour Scene and the Beach Boys. There was a strong British theme running through much of his favourite music and, alongside chuckling between themselves at Graham Coxon's accent, he and Adam bonded over their desire to emulate the Britpop sound. An incredulous Adam realised that, despite sharing countless classes with Jesse back home, he'd barely been aware of his existence before. All of this time, his musical soulmate had been right there under his nose.

He was also introduced to another Jesse, by the surname of Nicita. Back in LA, the trio – Adam on guitar and vocals, Jesse Carmichael on keyboards and Jesse Nicita on drums – recruited another Brentwood School student, Mickey Madden, to be their bassist.

Born on May 13, 1979, in Austin, Texas, Mickey had moved to LA early on and would later marvel that he owed his personality "almost entirely" to the culture he soaked up in the city. Yet in stark contrast to the archetypal American teenage boy, Mickey did not survive on a diet of football and video games. His tastes were more sophisticated – a passion for futuristic architecture and the art of Frank Stella, a fondness for the existential philosophy of Jean-Paul Sartre and an appetite for cult novelists such as Albert Camus and Vladimir Nabokov. The latter's controversial *Lolita* described falling in love with and seducing a pre-teen girl after the death of her mother – hardly average reading for a 13-year-old's bedside table, yet it was for Mickey.

His tastes in film were equally idiosyncratic, with the often psychologically sadistic thrillers of Roman Polanski among his favourites. "Mickey watched every movie that Polanski directed," revealed a former school friend to the author. "He loved Bond movies like anyone else his age, but he was also watching these mature, mentally stimulating films that most kids weren't ready for. For example, he loved *Rosemary's Baby*, a film about a woman whose husband belonged to a satanic cult. He fed her poisoned chocolate mousse, she fell unconscious and was raped by a demonic presence. Later she goes on to give birth to a devil child – it turned out that she'd been raped by Satan and if she wants to keep her baby, her only choice is to join the coven. It was horror, but it was never gore for its own sake – it was always twisted, cerebral and thought-provoking."

Rosemary's Baby followed the classic template of most of Polanski's films; Mickey also found himself drawn to the lesser known 1992 film *Bitter Moon*. In it, central character Mimi becomes dangerously addicted to an ill-fated love affair; when her partner tries to end it, she begs him not to leave. Sensing a way to exploit her neediness, desperation and vulnerability, he turns her into a reluctant masochist, agreeing to stay by her side only if he can attain total control. In one scene, he forces her to cut off all of her hair in a sadistic bid to destroy her beauty. Casually degrading her for his own amusement and perpetually nudging her boundaries out of a perverse curiosity to see just how far she'll go, he eventually tires of even a fully compliant Mimi and breaks away. Still riding on the ego-boosting wave of her devotion to him, he becomes a notorious womaniser, but misfortune – or perhaps karma – is ultimately inescapable.

Stumbling drunkenly out of a nightclub with a girl on each arm, he is struck down by a car accident that leaves him paralysed for life. Now confined to a wheelchair, his emotions at rock bottom, he is astonished when Mimi turns a blind eye to his past abuse and agrees to become his carer – but soon finds out why. The tables have turned on the power imbalance that characterised their relationship – now she is the all-powerful sadist who thrives on her partner's misery. On one occasion she leaves him crying out in pain in a scalding hot bath, all the while laughing and joking on the phone. She also forces him to listen forlornly in another room while she has sex with other men, revelling in his discomfort and compelling him to reflect on his lost sexuality.

More than a mere tale of revenge, *Bitter Moon* is filled with thought-provoking psychological twists that give an insight to the dark side of the human condition – something which Mickey had always been intrigued by. A deep thinker, his classmates considered him 'highbrow', uncommonly cerebral. He had a reputation for reading voraciously too – the books that most boys tolerated on their high school reading lists as a necessary evil in pursuit of the right grades were on Mickey's bookshelf by choice. He also had a sense of fun, however, combining wordy literature and serious cult classics with a penchant for implausible sci-fi plots. This would be the theme when he later joked of his journey from birth to professional bassist:

> "I burst forth from the womb fully grown and clad in armour back in 1979 and, having narrowly escaped the bulk of the Seventies, I began almost immediately on my search for identity. As it turns out, I'm actually a sophisticated class-3 android manufactured by an elite team of scientists and engineers and my thoughts and memory have been fabricated by a committee of writers and philosophers to suit the needs of the CIA. So, when I'm not inadvertently carrying out government orders, I play bass!"

Adam and the two Jesses gladly welcomed the 'android' into the fold as their fourth member, whereupon he added his own diverse musical tastes to the mix. The foursome already shared a love of the Rolling Stones, the Kinks, Sonic Youth, the Velvet Underground, the Clash and the entire genre of 'rebel rock', but while the others were addicted to pop and rock, Mickey balanced it out by introducing them to jazz, sixties soul and Motown. He loved Otis Redding, the Chiffons, the Supremes, the Crystals, the Ronettes, Stevie Wonder, James Brown, John Coltrane, Roy Eldridge and Ella Fitzgerald. His CD collection often referenced the days of excessive hairspray and bouffant beehives tall and eccentric enough to have put Amy Winehouse to shame. Yet above all, the constant theme was of passionate, heart-rending soul ballads, odes to unfaithful or drug-addicted lovers.

Its emphasis was in keeping with Mickey's unusual precociousness, but the emotionally loaded tracks weren't to everyone's tastes. As fellow former Brentwood student Paul Rumsey recalls to the author: "Before they could even begin, there was a massive argument over the sound. They were ridiculously talented, but let's not forget [three of them] were still teenage boys. They were getting serious very young and so, while they all wanted to nail a distinctive sound for their group and make it their own, they were having trouble agreeing on even the basics."

By this time, Jesse and Adam were inseparable, declaring themselves best friends who'd bonded by their shared love of rock music. Together, they eventually persuaded their bandmates that this was the right direction for the band – it was modern, fashionable and tapped into a trend that would persist throughout the nineties. At this time, Nirvana's grunge-rock classic 'Smells Like Teen Spirit' was enjoying a resurgence on seemingly every music channel, while Kurt Cobain's partner, Courtney Love, was paralleling his work via her own band, Hole. These were the early nineties, the days of Alanis Morissette, Green Day and Weezer – and the four boys' collective fantasy of becoming their icons' musical next-of-kin eventually became too irresistible to ignore.

Now they just needed a name. In contrast to the lengthy debate over their sound, the four quickly settled upon the bizarre moniker of Edible Nuns. "I think they were gently and wittily poking fun at the hypocrisy of the Christian religion," one anonymous childhood friend confided to the author. "Back then, there were sex scandals surrounding the church so the 'edible' part of the name was adding a lot of sexual innuendo, reflecting how dubious they were that nuns were actually as chaste as they seemed. Anyway at their age, they would rather have lost a leg than face the idea of never having sex again, so the name of Edible Nuns was just a tongue-in-cheek way of poking fun at it all – that whole incomprehensible lifestyle."

Next came the nerve-racking acid test for any group – their first live show. None of the teenagers had been onstage before with the exception of Adam who, at the tender age of 12, had performed a vocal rendition of 'Rockin' Robin' live at the LA Troubadour. He was assisting another friend, Adam Salzman, with his band Blurred Vision.

The three bandmates were petrified when it came to their inaugural show, playing Pearl Jam and Alice in Chains covers at their junior high school summer dance. Stage fright had hit Adam the hardest – he had all the qualities of an exhibitionist but, due to his appearance, was also painfully shy. Inside, there was a gregarious boy trying to break free, one who described himself as having "an almost unquenchable thirst to be the centre of attention" – but he couldn't live up to that description externally.

Adam possessed a thick, bushy mono-brow, inviting taunts about caterpillars living on his face. His hair was long, unkempt and straggly and his teeth slightly crooked. In what seemed like the ultimate curse for any would-be rock star, he had the appearance of an archetypal school geek. Like a child struggling miserably to walk in his father's oversized shoes, he just hadn't yet grown into the looks that would later make him a sex symbol.

Nature had thrown another curveball too: his face was smothered in acne. "He was so sensitive about his looks," one former friend told the author, "that he would play entire shows with his back turned to the audience."

Although friends, family and teachers alike were supportive, they were also sceptical – could a boy really make it in music when he couldn't even make eye contact with a high-school crowd? Adam felt their pitying glances; as he walked down corridors, their unspoken sympathy stung his pride. Yet he persevered and, as time went on, he started to conquer his stage fright.

However, Edible Nuns was short-lived. Just as Adam was getting more comfortable, Jesse Nicita left to pursue other projects. The resilient group instantly drafted in a female friend, Amy Wood, to take his place. Like the others she was 13, but already had five years of experience due to sitting in on her musician father's rehearsal sessions in his home studio. As the group was now officially one quarter female, they decided to name the new line-up Mostly Men.

Capitalising on the novelty value of their age and the rarity of a female drummer, they wasted no time in booking contacts at school and in the local area. Adam was soon hooked.

"I was a total dickhead," he would later recall, with disarming candour. "I didn't do any homework – I just went home and wrote music or played guitar or had band practice."

Adam may have been obsessed with music, milking the thrill of being a guitarist and lead singer – but his passion also acted as a convenient smokescreen for a growing problem: he was finding it increasingly difficult to focus. He was insatiably energetic, but struggled to channel his energy. Each thought, before he could even consciously process it, seemed to be interrupted by myriad others. It was like watching a TV that was simultaneously tuned in to dozens of channels, each one clashing with the others until all faded into a cacophony of unintelligible sound. It wasn't just annoying – it was debilitating.

"I [suffered] inattention, hyperactivity and impulsivity," Adam would later recall. "I don't think my peers noticed that I was different in any way but personally I struggled with academics, even though I knew I was fully capable of performing well in school . . . it was hard for me at times to sit down, focus and get school work done [and] I was frustrated."

There was clearly more to his dislike of school than lack of interest. To make matters worse, his parents had invested generously in his education, paying almost $30,000 per year in tuition fees; the cost of his schooling alone would have been enough (in less affluent areas of LA) to buy a small condo.

While there was no explicit pressure, there had been an unspoken expectation that, like his family, he would perform well academically and take a job that justified his parents' hefty financial sacrifice. The stakes were high: his relatives included bankers, high-profile political journalists,

TV producers and millionaire businessmen. Yet while there was a family tradition of graduating from top colleges such as Harvard and UCLA, Adam was beginning to doubt that he could even get through school.

Feeling guilty and conflicted, he eventually confided in his parents, who took him to the doctor. Expecting a simple course of pills to aid his concentration, he was shocked – and almost relieved – to discover his problem had a name. "What was helpful to me was learning that this was a real medical condition," he reflected later. "I had ADHD."

Every one of his difficulties was a classic attention deficit hyperactivity disorder symptom: attention lapses, boredom after spending just a few minutes on a task, trouble sitting still, a tendency to be disorganised and easily distracted and an inability even to concentrate on someone's speech. The condition is believed to be caused by an imbalance in neurotransmitters, chemicals responsible for transmitting nerve signals in the brain. Scans typically indicate under-activity in the areas of the brain that control inhibition, causing a flood of random thoughts to continuously overwhelm sufferers and compromise their ability to focus selectively. Patients also tend to show a reduced brain mass in the same areas.

Yet Adam had been right when he'd insisted he knew he had the potential to succeed in school – studies have suggested that when IQ in ADHD sufferers is tested verbally, they show an average 20-point lead on when the same pupil takes the test in a written format. It wasn't a cognitive deficit – the challenge lay simply in applying himself.

That said, the prognosis for sufferers wasn't good – in over a third of patients medication proves ineffective, while an estimated 10 million Americans continue to suffer the condition into adulthood. Even worse, statistics put Adam in a high-risk category for criminality, drug abuse and clinical depression. Cheered on by his supportive parents, he tentatively created a treatment plan based on the prescription drug Ritalin and a course of behavioural therapy – but what truly saved him was music.

Warding off bouts of rage and frustration, he found his guitar playing and singing had a therapeutic effect, calming him down and blessing him with focus when all else had failed. "Without it I think he would have gone over the edge," hypothesised one childhood friend. "Knowing what he wanted to do in life from an early age really helped."

From that point onwards, he was desperate to succeed in showbiz.

Together with childhood friend and future actor Jonah Hill – whose father had been best buddies with his own for decades – Adam would find the confidence to voice his ambitions. "I'm gonna be a rock star," he would insist with excitement, while Jonah would reply in kind: "I'm gonna be an actor."

At first glance, it was little more than boastful bravado – after all, what aspiring teen, especially with the inspiration of Hollywood as a backdrop, didn't dream of carving out a showbiz career? So many dreamt of it and yet so few succeeded – suffice to say that, in a world increasingly saturated with wannabes, the odds were not in his favour.

"The irony of Adam's success and my own success," Jonah would admit years later, "is that [growing up] we were both the least likely to succeed." In fact they were relentlessly ribbed by classmates, written off as losers and deluded fantasists – and yet both had an unwavering faith that one day it would happen.

Every tall tree had once been an insignificantly small seed; every man-made invention, before it could take shape, had started out as a fledgling idea in someone's head; every fully grown adult had once been a tiny foetus. Without the dreams there could be no reality.

Now the boys simply had to bridge the gap between potentiality and actuality. Adam's main reason for craving success was a love of music – but there were other factors too, and one such motivation was to avoid college. He didn't want to be forced by default into an education system that, due to his mental health struggles, would stifle and frustrate him. He knew academia was the wrong path for him and yet it was a proudly held family tradition and his conscience told him that, if he was going to abandon it, he needed an extremely viable alternative. A characteristically impatient Adam might have hated the fragile stage of being in limbo, but in many ways it was an exciting moment – any number of possibilities lay ahead, waiting to be realised.

Jonah remained a constant source of support to keep him on track and his enduring affection was reciprocated. In fact Adam described him as almost a member of his family. "He was a screwy kid like me," he would chuckle to *Details* magazine later. "We were both rebellious and didn't like school."

Another driving force for Adam – part of the reason he gravitated towards music – was the age-old fantasy of becoming more appealing to the opposite sex. He'd been spoilt endlessly at home by his doting mother and live-in mother-in-law, but his geeky appearance wasn't earning him the same adulation at school.

"I was very uncool," he confessed to *Paper*. "I had disgusting long hair and shorts down to my knees, cut-off shorts – I desperately wanted to be Eddie Vedder from Pearl Jam really badly but I was just a nerdy, awkward kid [who] was obsessed with music."

That was the vast gulf between fantasy and reality. Undeterred, the young hopeful created a shrine to Pearl Jam in his bedroom, plastering the walls with magazine clippings to keep tabs on his idol. Collating notes for future reference in his desired career was, much to the frustration of his parents, the closest Adam would ever get to homework.

In spite of his geeky appearance – normally a barrier to success with girls – he would be approached by intrigued female classmates keen to get the lowdown on his life as lead singer of a band. Although Brentwood High bred stars – with soon-to-be actors Jason Segel and Jake Gyllenhaal in his class – it was striking for someone to show showbiz credentials, no matter how modest, at the age of 13.

Another factor that contributed to his status as an unlikely stud was his maturity and experience with girls. While some of his peers blushed and stuttered their way through conversations with the opposite sex, painfully awkward and self-aware, Adam was a natural.

One of the biggest 'Men are from Mars, women are from Venus' stereotypes is that girls traditionally relish an opportunity to express themselves and discuss their feelings, while on average, men tend to speak far less and take a problem-solving (rather than emotional) approach to life. This is often exacerbated in teenage boys, who typically prefer video-games, horror movies and football matches to the dreaded art of self-expression.

Yet this was far from the case with Adam, who'd lived without an adult male presence in the house since he was seven, long enough to understand female psychology. Eager to please, he had tapped into their love of sensitivity and romantic gestures, traits that were rare among many of his hapless peers. He'd also heard his mother gripe about failed relationships enough to realise precisely which qualities a woman *didn't* want in a man.

"One of my theories on why I'm so capable of understanding women," Adam would later concur a little less than modestly, "is that . . . I was living in a house with two jilted women, plus my cousin, who's more like my sister. Just the oestrogen alone . . . you know when you're 14 and terrified to talk to a girl? I didn't suffer much from that. It seemed very natural to me to talk to girls!"

He also shared the house with his brother, Michael, who had recently confirmed the family wisdom that he was gay. "I can single-handedly dispel any ideas that sexuality is acquired," Adam later asserted to popular gay magazine *Out*. "Trust me, you're born with it. We knew [my brother was gay] when he was two. We all knew.

"We all really wanted to provide some cushion for him and constantly let him know that it's OK," Adam added. "A lot of people don't want their kid to be gay and will fight it at all costs. But I've got news for you – it's a losing fucking battle. The more you fight it, the more fucked up your kid's gonna be. You've just gotta embrace it from the beginning . . . otherwise you're just screwing yourself over and you're gonna make your kid miserable."

A committed liberal, it had never occurred to Adam to deny or question his brother's sexuality – let alone to scorn or tease him for it. Yet not everyone was so tolerant and Michael endured mild bullying for being effeminate. Adam would later wryly acknowledge that living with him had increased the oestrogen ratio even higher.

In spite of being a natural with girls, his burning competitive instinct compelled him to take things a step further by charming them with songs. How many of his classmates could compete with that?

By now Adam had gravitated from playing cover versions of his favourite rock songs to writing his own guitar tunes and lyrics – and he used his skill to maximum effect. While he almost needed to write to satisfy his creative instincts, it didn't escape his attention that his skills were good for matchmaking.

"If I really liked a girl and I felt these romantic feelings towards her," he would later reflect, "I would literally write a song and make sure she heard it. It was so bold . . . [but] I didn't have money or a job. All I had was a girl I was in love with and the dream of being a famous musician."

23

2

Signed

ADAM's all-consuming passion for music was replicated by Jesse and Mickey – but the trio were sceptical about Amy. "I was terrible," she would exclaim later – and embarrassingly, her bandmates didn't disagree. She would go on to become a little-known session musician, but the other members of Mostly Men – by now all 14 – knew they had to part ways with her.

In those days, they lived and breathed music, almost needing it to survive. It was akin to an addictive love affair or a dalliance with drugs – but, thankfully, far less toxic. Yet while the three boys were in it for the long haul, Amy lacked their obsession, commitment and, some might say, musical competence. The separation meant that Mostly Men were now only men – or, in reality, teenage boys.

Unsure of their next step, their saving grace was Adam's friend Ryan Dusick, who had befriended him back after his winning shot in basketball, aged six – a coup that had turned him into a miniature celebrity in school. The pair had drifted apart, but Jesse reconnected them when, at a high school pep rally, he challenged Ryan to join them on drums for a rehearsal of the Alice in Chains song 'Them Bones'. "He'd never played with us before," Jesse would recall, "but we knew of him as the cool drummer who was two years older than us – as in 16, as in a driver. Very cool."

The trio were almost in awe of Ryan and would strive to make their musical jams a regular event. He shared their love of the Beatles, Stevie Wonder, Pearl Jam and Weezer, but also introduced them to such diverse acts such as XTC, Van Halen, Soundgarden, Led Zeppelin, Ben Folds Five, Sugarplastic and early Smashing Pumpkins.

Ryan would be forced to apologise to his bandmates, however, for his love of much ridiculed TV comedy show *Beavis & Butthead*: "I am a huge fan . . . [but] I think a lot of people don't understand that it's a satire. A lot of people either think it's moronic or they think it's funny because they identify with it. Either way, you're missing the boat."

Questionable TV tastes aside, the foursome soon realised that they had a unique musical chemistry, via renditions of tracks like Soundgarden's 'Black Hole Sun'. The cerebral Mickey, according to Adam, the group's "musical encyclopaedia" instantly clicked with the older and equally mature Ryan, but in fact all four realised there was a magical *je ne sais quoi* about the new line-up, something they had formerly lacked. Perhaps it was third time lucky.

High on adrenalin and unable to sleep after a memorable concert, Jesse, Adam and Ryan secretly crept out of the latter's parents' house, where they were due to spend the night, and embarked on an adventure that, within hours, would end with the formation of a *real* group (not merely a bunch of kids that played covers) called Kara's Flowers.

"On that fateful February 6 of the year 1994, we snuck out, after an evening of inspirational Hollywood music at the Troubadour on Santa Monica Blvd," Jesse recalled. "This was the first time Adam and Ryan and I had *really* all hung out together and we were deciding that night to form a band."

During conversation, all four admitted to a mutual infatuation with a classmate named Kara, who just so happened to be turning 15 that night. Spurred on by illicitly drunken bravado and led by Adam, the teenage king of romantic gestures, they decided to document their devotion in a way she was sure to remember.

"We purchased some flowers from a street-walking flower vendor, at 3:00 in the morning," Jesse chuckled fondly, "and somehow found Kara's house using our school directory, information service and a Hollywood map. Then we delivered the flowers and a note confessing that we all thought Kara was 'beatiful'. I wrote the note – how cute is it that I misspelled beautiful? Adorable. And as you might have guessed, this was the night that Kara's Flowers the band was formed."

The average teenage boy might have been despondent, because the much-in-demand Kara steadfastly refused to date any of them. On the plus side, however, they now had a mission – and a name that defined it. The following morning, the trio filled Mickey in as he pledged allegiance to them as bassist. Their group was now complete – and for the first time the chemistry felt just right.

From that moment forth they practised obsessively, building up a playlist of songs. By the summer, they were ready for their debut recording session. It happened almost accidentally: the quartet found themselves in the house of Noah Gershman – later to become a professional poet but back then a lowly Brentwood High School student like the rest of them – and, with a little encouragement from their host, proceeded to record an 11-track demo right there in Noah's basement.

Ryan and Adam had collaborated on the majority of the writing, but the resulting material was what a shame-faced Mickey would later describe as overly "heavy and brooding", and filled with nonsensical lyrics. Examples of these early songs included 'Clomb', 'Miner', 'Stable' and the nondescript 'Untitled'.

Other tracks gave a clue to their tender age, laced as they were with mischief and humour. For instance, 'Leave A Message' was prefaced by the sound of the boys animatedly arguing before Ryan took on the vocals, comically begging a mystery caller to phone him back. Then there was 'Dame Cabeza', an audacious ode to oral sex – the title was inspired by the Spanish slang phrase for "give me head", with Adam talking of wanting to use someone and forthrightly exclaiming during the chorus that all he wanted was "your head".

While 'Give Me Love' might have seemed like a continuation of the same theme, in fact it tapped into the self-doubt, shame and depression of some of the best-loved grunge-rock artists of their era. Many of them were tortured souls who wrote because they had to – they felt chronically misunderstood and used music as therapy to release their frustration. For example Nirvana had spawned tracks such as 'Lithium', named after a mood-stabilising antidepressant drug. Just as Kurt Cobain had proclaimed in song that he hated himself and wanted to die, Adam claimed in his own lyrics that he felt he might as well be dead. This was doubtless what Mickey had meant when he described the melancholic material as "brooding".

"[Kara's Flowers] weren't really depressed, other than the usual teenage hormones," one old school friend divulges to the author, "but it was considered fashionable at that time in their musical genre to talk about self-destructive instincts and suicide." That same song also described a textbook case of ambivalent love, when Adam sang of a need to keep his partner close but, seconds later, urged her to stay away.

It wasn't just Nirvana that the group used for inspiration; the tracks 'Mental Mind Fuck' and 'Ray Pim' were strongly influenced by Green Day who, in February 1994 (just a few months before the Kara's Flowers demos were recorded), had released their fourth album, *Dookie*, to enormous acclaim.

Since the eighties, the group had been signed to an obscure independent record label, Lookout!, which specialised in punk rock and operated out of Berkeley, California. With limited funding behind them and few serious corporate connections, the label owners were motivated by sheer passion for their genre – but in an increasingly competitive music scene, their enthusiasm didn't translate to sales.

Following three successful underground albums, Green Day tired of niche notoriety and began to crave popularity, yearning for mainstream music fans to hear their sound. When they were scouted by Reprise – a major label imprint of Warner Bros Records that offered more resources, more exposure and, of course, a larger pay cheque – the temptation was irresistible and they switched allegiances straight away.

Almost overnight, they became a punk rock phenomenon, with the first single from *Dookie*, 'Longview', hitting number one on the *Billboard* rock chart. Reprise had a larger marketing budget and, before long, almost everyone in Green Day's target audience had heard their name – Adam included.

"I remember hearing Green Day for the first time and being kind of blown away," he would later recall to *ABC News*. "When I heard 'Longview' on the radio, I was just kind of enamoured by it. I was like, 'Wow, what's this?' It was very accessible, melodic rock'n'roll music, but it was a little pissed off and obnoxious."

In the years to come, he would offer direct praise to Green Day by writing: "Thank you for always making the best 'I'm wearing headphones and ignoring your bullshit' records I can ignore the world with."

That sentiment summed up the very essence of Green Day's music – an attitude of rebellion, defiance and anti-authority politics, all delivered against the backdrop of a middle-finger salute. 'Longview', the song that had symbolised their breakout success, was a protest of intense boredom. "It was just living in the suburbs in a sort of shit town where you can't even pull in a good radio station," lead singer Billie Joe Armstrong would later tell *Guitar Legends* of his source of inspiration. "I was living in Rodeo, California, about 20 minutes outside of Oakland. There was nothing to do there and it was a real boring place."

The song, which Billie had written under the influence of LSD, described endless days whiled away with excessive marijuana smoking and masturbation. Confessing that he was smoking away his inspiration, he delivered a straight-talking slice of candour, expressing sentiments that the average blue or white-collar worker might feel but would be too petrified to admit.

Adam was magnetically drawn to his blunt honesty, which was entirely fitting to the punk rock mindset. He could also relate to his idol's earlier struggle to climb the rock'n'roll ladder, as he desperately strived to be on the radio himself but was feeling frustratingly impotent in those pre-fame days. He might have been able to enact his fantasies of celebrity standing in Noah's cramped basement and singing his heart out to a battered old tape deck, but the illusion was painfully fleeting – and once the music stopped, he faced an inevitable return to reality. All the demands of academia would come flooding back, the pressure of writing endless essays and feigning interest in school despite his conviction that he would rather die than let go of a career in music.

While his home corner of California was more exciting than Billie Joe Armstrong's, he couldn't shake the feeling that he was merely killing time until he 'made it' – and the worst part of all was his uncertainty over whether that day would ever come. It was with this dilemma in mind that he and Ryan penned 'Ray Pim'; just as 'Longview' had done before it, the track tapped into loneliness, isolation and boredom, and the pain of as yet unrealised dreams.

Meanwhile, 'Mental Mind Fuck' emulated the theme of masturbation in 'Longview'. In the latter, Billie wryly remarks that while his mother is pressuring him to get a job, she doesn't even like her own – so why follow her example? Loath to spend a lifetime as a corporate slave, he's holding out for his dream but doesn't know how to make it happen. In the absence of a route map, he resorts to the easier prospect of masturbating repeatedly out of pure boredom, while poking fun at warnings that he'll go blind. Inspired, Adam then channelled his angst into his own version of the song. Littering it with random, abstract or at times comical lyrics *à la* Frank Zappa or Ian Dury, he laments that he has "nothing but a tangent" – and one that will distract him from music.

While Green Day was now an established group and the album that inspired Adam had already sold in its millions, the two had more in common than first met the eye. Both shared an experience – one current and one historical – of frustration and alienation as they tried to hit the big time. Green Day had also endured a dilemma that struck a chord with Adam – whether to remain loyal to their financially crippled former label and be the eternally unsung underground artists, or to take the plunge with a major label that could transform their anonymity and change their lives.

While the answer might seem obvious, on the alternative scene, where the group had attained their early cult fame, there were often negative connotations attached to mainstream success. They risked being perceived as sell-outs who'd contemptibly abandoned their roots in pursuit of profit and, in the process, lost the respect of the very people they'd originally entered the business to attract.

Alt-rock groups often appealed to a minority who felt alienated from society, as though they didn't belong. They provided anthems that gave validation to square pegs in round holes. Yet by becoming part of a major mainstream corporation, Green Day ran the risk of distancing themselves from their oldest fans and beginning to represent everything they once despised.

Clearly, the naysayers would always be possessive over 'their' group, but there was more to their concerns than that – there were worries that Green Day might sacrifice their integrity. Could they sell out without selling their souls?

Signing with a major label conventionally came with the risk of losing creative control and, if stereotypes were to be believed, it also meant being cynically manufactured and marketed to maximum profit until their real selves had been airbrushed out of the picture. When *Dookie* was released, however, its politically incorrect, family-unfriendly anthems of masturbation and opposition to authority demonstrated that the true heart of the group had not been lost. But Kara's Flowers didn't want to take that chance.

"The way [the music industry] is set up, the artist gets screwed in comparison to the record label," Mickey would warn later. "The balance is very tipped in the record label's favour . . . there's so much *business* to the music business that the scales are tipped in favour of money as opposed to art, because you can count money. It's a tangible, quantifiable thing and art is much more abstract, so you can't really put a price on it."

"When you sign a record contract," Ryan concurred, "it's a negotiation that's one-sided . . . an unfair balance." Mickey's final words of warning were unambiguous: "Don't suck corporate dick. Don't sell out."

This was exactly the dilemma Adam had in mind when he wrote 'Peeler'. "He was always two steps ahead," recalled one school friend. "He didn't even have a deal yet and he was already picturing himself in Green Day's shoes, imagining making the choice between two very different labels. 'Peeler' was all about peeling away from the crowd and doing his own thing – so that gives you an idea [of], in their place, which road he would have chosen."

Sure enough, the lyrics sneered at someone who does "as you've been told" and is consequently "killing" their future, reaffirming Kara's Flowers' commitment to uniqueness and opposition to conformity. In a world saturated by manufactured music, they were keen to stay true to their sound.

Finally, 'Genius' was one of the most mature tracks on the demo tape. Unlike the hastily arranged and, at face value, often nonsensical lyrics of other songs – which spoke, for example, of "stocking the food of love and hate" – 'Genius' was serious and meaningful. It featured a woman who had abandoned Adam and left him feeling "unwanted" but had since returned for sentimental goodbye sex. Seizing the upper hand finally, Adam responds by telling her he won't meet as he doesn't care for "the last time" and vengefully anticipates her reaction when he makes it big in showbiz.

That concluded the first Kara's Flowers demo. However, their first effort suffered from the usual limitations of recording in someone's basement. In some songs, Adam's words were buried under the more dominant, heavily distorted sound of the instruments. The tracks were raw, imperfect and unpolished, but this early incarnation of Maroon 5 was aimed purely at capturing their energy and signature sound on tape. Even with the crackly undertone of Noah's paltry recording equipment, nothing could detract from the fact that they'd just taken a respectable first step.

The group christened their tape with the bizarre moniker *We Like Digging*, decorated it with photos of themselves in action and started distributing copies for free on the West Hollywood club scene. The only obvious barrier to success was their age – with seven years to go until they turned 21, they weren't legally allowed into nightclubs and bars. Regarded as just one of many wannabe bands in the city that defined showbiz, they were rarely taken seriously as performers. Smothered by red tape and stereotypes, the foursome had to hope that the demos would open doors that their unusually young appearance had sealed closed.

They did begin to make a small profit selling the tape to teachers and friends in their common room. As word spread, the sales tally slowly reached 500. Yet as the hype built around school, the boys felt obligated to provide the next instalment, celebrating the landmark sales figure by scheduling another recording.

Like start-up businessmen, they poured all of their initial profits back into their dream. This time, they weren't restricted to an amateur tape in their friend's basement – their success, as modest as it was, had afforded them a recording slot at local studio Room 222.

Adam, however, now nominated as the group's primary songwriter, was consumed by fears of failure. He was painfully aware that he was no longer writing for himself, but for a pre-existing audience – all of whom, in his mind, were waiting for songs that surpassed, or at least lived up to, their predecessors. The pressure to please them sent him into creative paralysis. The more he wanted to succeed, the more he succumbed to writer's block – and he found nothing more frustrating than staring at a blank page.

"This success was the beginnings of what they'd always wanted," a school friend who proudly kept his copy of *We Like Digging* revealed to the author. "Yet that success ironically put them under even more pressure. It's as if before he was singing whatever he wanted, oblivious to who might have heard, and then it all suddenly went silent and every head in the room had turned to look at what he was doing. It was as tense as a game of Russian roulette in that studio. It was make or break time and they literally felt like their next move would dictate whether they, as a band, would live or die."

Kara's Flowers was a team and yet Adam, as its frontman, bore the brunt of public scrutiny. To make matters worse, he was still struggling with ADHD. Thoughts and ideas would pop into his head constantly, only to disappear from his consciousness seconds later, before he could make use of them. When he tried to explain a concept to his bandmates it would often stay on the tip of his tongue, just out of reach. He lost his thoughts as quickly as Lehman Brothers lost cash; the more significant his ideas, the less able he felt to express them. Studio time was tightly structured and expensive, but he couldn't force creativity to flow within a fixed time-frame and his inhibitions were intensified by the ticking clock.

Nothing summed up that situation more aptly than 'Dream-maker #222'. The title was a reference to the name of the studio, the band wryly reflecting that their time there could make or break their dreams. The lyrics made brief mention of a girl who hadn't returned Adam's calls, but the writing leapt from subject to subject chaotically. It was characteristic of his struggle to focus his thoughts sufficiently to form a verse. By the end, the deficit was filled by Adam simply lamenting, "Where is the verse?" Unable to write naturally and unselfconsciously, he complained of feeling too "rehearsed" before repeatedly berating himself again.

'Angela' featured bizarre lyrics about sitting in a circle made of mud; 'On My Show' was a tribute devised by Adam to a girl he loved so much that she was famous in his eyes – and perpetually "on my show". Like the previous track, it was an ode to a crush on a local Brentwood girl. Finally, the group created 'Need Some Fun', featuring a clichéd but fun astrological theme – Adam sang of chasing moonbeams, falling out of the sky like a comet and staring at the sun.

In spite of the faltering lyrics, the four-track taster was well received. As the group gradually grew in confidence, they made plans to return to the studio a third time. On New Year's Eve, they agreed to perform at a friend's house party in Malibu to see in 1995, but, before they dragged their instruments there, they were booked in for a couple of hours of recording at Room 222.

The group committed three songs to tape, which continued their run of strangely opaque lyrics. In 'Pantry Queen', Adam sang that the boys were "digging the ground" and trying to stop it from reclaiming the unnamed treasures they'd found. 'Loving The Small Time' sounded heavily influenced by Smashing Pumpkins' 'Today'. Beneath cryptic lyrics about a "magic place" that was "nearing hell", it was more literally an ode to hitting the small time and the thrills of finding local success. While the sound gave a nod of appreciation to groups like Jimmy Eat World and Blink 182, the most obvious influence was Green Day. In the final track of the session, 'Future Kid', they proved it by referencing cartoon characters – their idols were, of course, famous for doing exactly the same.

In one of his moments of mind-numbing boredom in small-town Rodeo, Billie Joe Armstrong had happened upon an episode of children's TV show *Sesame Street*. As he watched, a roll-up dangling from his lips, a phrase jumped out at him: "I'm having a green day." Although the characters were undoubtedly referring to something more innocent, for the marijuana-loving Billie it was a shout-out to his favourite drug. In honour of the show, he and his bandmates featured cuddly Muppet character Ernie on the back cover of *Dookie*, rising out of a mosh pit. Yet when the album went 16 times platinum – a breakout success they could never have predicted – it quickly attracted the attention of *Sesame Street*'s producers, for whom the image of Ernie superimposed into the crowd of a Green Day show, rocking out, was too much to bear.

To some, Green Day already had a dubious reputation – they were politically correct advocates of mind-altering substances and partial to a little androgynous eyeliner. Yet to strait-laced parents, particularly in America's sizeable Bible belt, they were even more than that – they were an earthly manifestation of Satan himself. And so, before *Sesame Street*'s bosses could act, the parents did the talking for them. Ludicrously, it seemed some mothers had mistaken the tape for an official *Sesame Street* product – and when they found the polar opposite of a collection candy-coated children's songs, they were outraged.

"A few mums had bought their kids *Dookie*, thinking it was a children's record because it had Ernie from *Sesame Street* on the sleeve," Billie later recalled, barely able to conceal his amusement. "When their toddlers were listening to punk, they got angry. We had to take poor Ernie off because we got so much shit from parents."

Kara's Flowers were equally amused. In a nod to the episode, they'd later tell interviewers their sound was a cross between Fugazi, System Of A Down and *Sesame Street*. Yet on 'Future Kid', they teasingly took their references to cartoon characters a step further, claiming that Teddy Ruxpin, iconic talking teddy bear of eighties TV, was "a whore". When the song hit the shops a couple of years later, a reviewer from online music site *Popdose* would observe admiringly: "An infinite number of Michael Stipes at an infinite number of typewriters couldn't pen lyrics this comically obtuse."

It wasn't the first time that the squeaky-clean Teddy Ruxpin was referenced in the punk world either. The show was one of the very first Western cartoons to infiltrate Bulgaria, and the post-punk band Review had responded by releasing a song in Teddy Ruxpin's name. Meanwhile, Bulgaria's first underground music shop, MAVO, was named after the Monsters & Villains Organisation seen in the show. By now veritable punk historians, Kara's Flowers certainly seemed to have done their research.

★ ★ ★

On New Year's Eve 1994, the band's hard work would pay off.

Within hours of recording their three-track demo, the tireless group drove down to the beachside house party in Malibu at which they'd agreed to perform. As fate would have it, independent music producer Tommy Allan was walking his dog down the beach that evening – and when he heard the distant sound carried on the wind, he hurried over to investigate.

"Tommy was so taken by what he was hearing that he walked up to the door and introduced himself," his business partner, John DeNicola, tells the author, "and was surprised to find that they were 15 years old!"

John and Tommy, both experienced songwriters, had created a bicoastal production company, Omad, with the aim of scouting for new talent. After catching a glimpse of Kara's Flowers, New York-based John was the first person Tommy called. Barely able to contain himself, he began "raving" about their rare combination of youth and talent – right there on the doorstep of their friend's house.

Allan took an almost intuitive liking to their youthful energy and, as he listened closely, suspected that, beneath the teenage angst, predictable grunge-rock clichés and uninspired lyrics was enormous talent waiting to be harnessed. They sounded raw and unsophisticated, but that was exactly the same ingredient that made them so irresistible.

In the days that followed, he forwarded a copy of their demo tapes on to DeNicola, who likewise recognised their potential – in fact, he was drawn to them so much that he would soon join Tommy on a bid to make them famous.

"Within months, I flew out to LA, where we booked a recording session at Rumbo Studios and recorded six songs in one day as a trial to see if we all liked each other," John told the author.

Rumbo was a legendary LA studio nestled in the heart of the San Fernando Valley – but its modest, unassuming appearance in a deceptively quiet street gave no clue to the hedonistic antics that took place in its privacy. Over the years, No Doubt, Poison, Rage Against The Machine and Smashing Pumpkins had recorded multi-platinum albums there – and it had even received a visit from the slightly hapless Ringo Starr – but its most notorious residency was that of Guns N' Roses, whose aptly titled 1987 album, *Appetite For Destruction*, took shape at the address.

Guns N' Roses were arguably one of the hardest partying and most debauched rock bands of all time, and more than one band member was in the grip of heroin and cocaine, making writing sessions hugely chaotic. It would be their debut album but, even before the world knew their names, the boys – who Kara's Flowers held in great esteem – were already living up to every rock'n'roll cliché.

On the carnally fuelled 'It's So Easy', lead singer Axl Rose decided to make the mood authentic by featuring the real-time sounds of sex – with the help of a few willing groupies. An employee was later quoted as saying, "Axl fucked two or three girls at least two or three times at Rumbo, without being satisfied with the result."

One might suspect Axl was prolonging the sessions not to perfect the audio, but to capitalise on the perks of having sex while still legitimately working. Nonetheless, he could be heard on one demo berating his one-time partner for "faking it" and coaxing, "Come on, Adriana – make it real!"

Such was the history of this unassuming little studio that Kara's Flowers were feverish with excitement on arrival – and their enthusiasm showed. "They all played really well, each one of them – and their original songs were really fleshed out, especially for 15-year-olds," John DeNicola told the author. "They had a unique guitar-based sound with great vocals and excellent playing.

"Though they sounded indie, they didn't sound Seattle," he adds, referring to the birthplace of a thriving grunge and alt-rock scene which counted Nirvana, Soundgarden and Pearl Jam among its heroes. "They were melodic and more reminiscent of the sixties, but with a heavy guitar attack. This was 1995, a little before younger artists were so prevalent, so they were unusual."

Back then, Kara's Flowers was indisputably a guitar-driven rock band, with both Adam and Jesse – who had not yet taken up the keyboards – sharing out guitar duties equally. "The interplay between Adam and Jesse's guitars," John noted, "was stellar and electrifying."

Yet the Rumbo sessions served purely to produce professional recordings of some of the original demos – and, of course, to test their working chemistry with the men who thought they could make them stars. Keen to take the band further, John and Tommy then financed a long stint at the nearby Sound City Studios, the very location where Nirvana had recorded *Nevermind*. With a past clientele also including Metallica, Slipknot, Queens Of The Stone Age, Rage Against The Machine, Nine Inch Nails and Red Hot Chili Peppers, it was the studio of choice for many aspiring rockers. (After its closure in 2011, it would become the subject of a Dave Grohl-produced documentary.)

In the nineties, Rumbo had a special aura about it – and the band would bond easily with their producers there. "Tommy and I had a blast recording and writing with these guys," John fondly reminisced. "They were experiencing and talking about typical 15-year-old guy stuff – girls, school, partying. It was great fun watching and participating in their youthful exuberance and it created a wonderful energy in the studio. Every day we would send out for Good Humour Choco Tacos – that was a band staple throughout the recording! We all had our families around too. My wife and young son flew out and spent time with us at the studio and we got to meet and know all of the band members' parents."

In working with Kara's Flowers, Tommy and John vicariously experienced a kind of second youth. In turn, the band benefited from the wisdom and experience the duo had to offer them – although John is adamant that they didn't need any assistance in writing their material.

"Being a songwriter myself," he continued, "I was impressed with the band's songs and felt like they didn't need my help in that department. They were clearly onto something all on their own. As experienced musicians, Tommy and I have a very artist/musician point of view as producers, which entails knowing when to get out of the way and when to step in."

DeNicola's opinion was qualified by experience. He'd co-written the 1987 track '(I've Had) The Time Of My Life', which served as lead single from the 20-million selling soundtrack of the film *Dirty Dancing*. The album would stay at the top of the charts for 17 weeks and John's writing would be acknowledged by an Academy Award and a Golden Globe award, as well as a Grammy nomination. To further cement the song's status as a timeless classic, it would later be sampled by the Black Eyed Peas in the form of 'The Time (Dirty Bit)', combining the melody of the original song with new music and enjoying similar success as a number one hit.

Not wanting to intervene and spoil the magic that had built up in the group, John sat back, transfixed, as song after song began to unfold. "The lyrics were obtuse and open to interpretation and fantastical," he recalls. "There were themes of aliens, science fiction, carnivals and other boyish teenage fantasies with clever lyrical turns. It was a sort of science fiction tale, but it wasn't real – it was sort of implied. The songs were held together by a common youth-driven storyline."

They produced an updated version of 'Future Kid', alongside the similarly themed 'Revenge Of The Kill Toys'. Inspired by a combination of *Dr Who* serial 'The Celestial Toymaker' and a number of horror movies the boys had seen, it depicted children's toys coming to life and vengefully waging war on their owners for treating them like property.

Also linked to 'Future Kid' was 'The Never Saga', a science fiction tale about a woman who'd been snatched by aliens and was waiting for "future's child" to save her. The two tracks formed part of a trilogy with 'Soap Disco' – another fantastical story that many people would misinterpret on release. "You know those discos in New York and Europe where they fill up the floor with soap bubbles?" Mickey would later observe. "A lot of people think it's about that!"

"It was about the triumphant kids that 'overthrew the slime'," John told the author, "and it was like a carnival barker saying, 'Check it out, see what it's all about.' Soap Disco – see the world from a cleaner point of view."

Then there was 'Captain Splendid' and its maritime theme, prompted by what Mickey would describe as "Adam's lyrical fascination with boats and oceans and storms". It depicted the life of a sailor in the navy who'd lost his leg in battle and had suffered crippling loneliness ever since because, according to Adam, no one cared for "ocean affairs". The comically titled 'Sleepy Windbreaker' continued the sea theme with its stories of sailors "taking a stand".

Yet while many of the lyrics depicted outlandish fantasy stories, there was a depth to the recordings as well. One track with a more serious side was 'Myself'. Even at their tender ages, growing up a stone's throw from Hollywood meant the group didn't lack knowledge of the sordid side of showbiz. They'd seen enormously talented actors and musicians crumble after succumbing to drug addiction, and 'Myself' was an ode to the difficulties of staying afloat in an industry rife with temptation. The track spoke of someone who was offered "remedies" struggling to maintain self-control; having previously "choked" on these remedies, he stands his ground, insisting that, even if he ends up lonely as a result of his abstinence, at least he'll have his health.

'To Her With Love' was surprisingly tender for boys of their age. Promising to support someone's dream, Adam sings appreciatively that even roses and diamonds could not take the place of his lover's face. Another love song, 'Oliver', took on the perspective of the title character from the musical based on *Oliver Twist*. The track, jokingly described later as "a sequel to the musical, with less acting", recalls the impoverished boy's love for Nancy, the woman who tried to protect him when he was wanted for a burglary, only to be murdered by her partner, Bill, for her troubles.

The group also re-recorded 'Loving The Small Time', 'Pantry Queen' and 'Ray Pim', to complete a full 12-track album. John and Tommy then recruited producer friend Ed Stasium, also known for his work with Living Colour, the Ramones, Smithereens and Gladys Knight, to bring the album to life after the boys had completed the initial sessions.

Yet as recording drew to a close, John became acutely aware that the band's potential was greater than the reach of a small independent label. Increasingly, he felt that they could benefit from the attention of a larger, more well-established record company with widespread contacts and better financial backing. Envisaging international success in the right hands, he and Tommy decided not to release the album themselves. Rather, they would take on an informal management role in the boys' future, working to negotiate a deal with a mainstream label.

"When we realised that the band could go beyond the indie market and possibly flourish in a larger context, we decided to shop it to the major labels," John says, "but while some labels responded well, some didn't hear it."

One particular curveball was the evolution of the group's sound. "The core of our material [was initially] heavy and brooding," Mickey would reveal, "[but] after a year or so of this, our tastes were changing, as they so often do at that tender age, and we entered a phase of massive, obsessive Beatlemania that culminated in some ill-advised matching suits and big, bright pop songs with loud guitars."

Friend Jake Gyllenhaal was impressed when he caught them on the LA club scene in their Beatles-inspired pinstripe suits – but record labels were less enchanted. Quite simply, it didn't tap into the trend of the moment. "A lot of music at the time was grunge/Seattle-influenced," John clarified, "and as Kara's Flowers was more Beatles/sixties-inspired, some labels did not get it."

The search continued, while some encouraging words from musical veteran David Crosby raised their morale. Crosby was an LA-born singer-songwriter and guitarist who'd once seen his debut solo album reach number 12 on the *Billboard* chart. He'd performed in a succession of bands, including Crosby, Stills & Nash who often shared a stage with Neil Young. He also had an infamously colourful history, including serving prison time for weapons charges. After one of his multiple misdemeanours, a reporter had questioned why police officers had found cocaine and a pistol in his car – only to be met with the bizarre response "John Lennon, man!" He would repeat the phrase as an answer to every question posed.

Yet his wild days were behind him by the late nineties and he'd shown far more clarity towards Kara's Flowers. His response convinced them that, although their sound might not translate to success in everyone's eyes, the most important thing was to record on their own terms.

"It was at a lunch meeting at the Beverly Hills Hotel, with the band and a label A&R guy," John DeNicola recalled, "and we ran into David in the lobby. One of the band members' parents knew him and we were telling him about what we were doing, recording the record and then shopping it. He said how great it was not to be at the label's mercy creatively, to do the record the way we all wanted it without a major label's input."

While there were still sprinklings of Green Day ever present in the Kara's Flowers sound, the band also showed their fair share of diversity. Without a profit-hungry mogul from a mainstream label nudging them in a preconceived commercial direction, the result might not have been to everyone's tastes – but at least they'd stayed true to their own unique sound.

Exchanging words with David Crosby was almost more important than meeting with the A&R rep they'd originally arrived to see. It proved a turning point – they could either mould themselves into a carbon copy of every other post-grunge group, coldly calculating their sound for the maximum chance of success, or they could continue deviating from the norm and perhaps become trendsetters instead. It was a bold move, but in time they might even be able to dictate the sounds of the future – a far more exciting prospect than following the herd.

The group's audience slowly increased and, on September 16, 1995, they played their first formal show at the Whisky A Go Go, a 1,000-capacity rock club on the Sunset Strip in West Hollywood. It made for a good beginning, having once played host to the Animals, Led Zeppelin, Janis Joplin and the Doors, while Iggy & The Stooges had formerly taken the club by storm with a five-night-stand.

Not only were prospective fans present, but John and Tommy had used their contacts to net the group some valuable exposure. Before long, two major labels – Epic and Atlantic – made their introduction. For them, part of the group's appeal lay in the contrast between their ages and the maturity of the sound. Being 15 was, in itself, a novelty in the music industry – prior to the days of *The X Factor*, teenage self-starters had been few and far between. Yet they also had a distinct sound – and the only sonic clue that betrayed their age was the flamboyancy of the lyrics, combining hard-hitting punk pop with theatrical science fiction and tales of killer teddy bears. They were a rare find indeed.

After an invitation from their headmaster to perform on school premises, an even bigger twist was to follow. Compared to a 1,000-capacity nightclub and the interest of two major labels, a subsequent concert in the Brentwood High School gym seemed like small fry – but it was a show that would change their lives.

"They played 'Tomorrow' by Silverchair and Beatles songs," Brentwood school friend Mark James recalled of that evening, "and they had lit candles around them, all over the floor."

Yet unbeknown to them, a high-profile producer was hiding in the audience. As the scene unfolded, Rob Cavallo – the man who masterminded Green Day's *Dookie* – was transfixed. Undeterred by the raw, low-budget quality of the show, he saw similarities in Kara's Flowers that reminded him of his younger self – especially when they broke into Beatles songs.

"I got a stack of Beatles records when I was 11," Rob later recalled. "I had to know how they were making those sounds. I learned how to play their entire catalogue on every instrument the way they did. I learned how to play the guitar, bass, drums, piano and everything. I became a student of musical production and sonics. Then I did the same thing with the Rolling Stones, the Who, Led Zeppelin and every hit from the last 50 years."

After a short-lived stint in a punk group, Rob had decided performance "wasn't in his DNA" and instead threw himself into production behind the scenes full time at Warner Bros Records imprint Reprise. After transforming Green Day from a low-key underground act with a small cult following to a worldwide punk-rock phenomenon, he was promoted to Senior Vice President – and that's when he came across Kara's Flowers.

His friend, Third Rail manager Pat Magnarella, had heard their demo tape and passed it onto Cavallo, who was now interested in getting involved with their career. Rob approached the group straight after the show, but he and Pat were offering themselves as a package; if Kara's Flowers accepted, it meant that John and Tommy could no longer manage them.

Yet staying with the latter would have been an enormous leap of faith –

the only guarantee they could give was a place on a small independent label which, in spite of its owners' best intentions, lacked the financial clout to propel them into a worldwide market. Reprise, on the other hand, seemed to offer the same flexibility and creative control as their former neighbour – a rarity on a major label – but with the added bonus that they seemed to have the right tools at their fingertips to make the boys into stars.

To gauge whether Reprise could potentially offer both mainstream success and individual freedom, Kara's Flowers needed look no further than their ultimate idols: Green Day. They'd moved to the label because, while they had no wish to compromise the rebellion-fuelled rock for which they were famed, they didn't want a career of permanent underground obscurity either. They felt they deserved to move beyond mere cult idolisation into the mainstream, asking for the world at large to hear their voice.

It seemed Reprise could offer a workable compromise – the group went on to sell over 10 million copies of *Dookie* stateside, but without sacrificing any of their artistic credibility. Instead of trying to change their trademark sound, Reprise had championed their existing one – and they'd become a breakout success without deferring to a formula. That was exactly the type of career trajectory that Kara's Flowers hoped to replicate.

Reprise's roots were firmly founded in artistic freedom too. The label had originally been a vehicle for Frank Sinatra's work, the singer having founded it back in 1960, and his goal had been creative control. After he sold it on to Warner Bros, artists such as Jimi Hendrix and Primal Scream had achieved success via the label – but most important for Adam, Mickey, Jesse and Ryan was the affiliation with Green Day.

That was the deciding factor – and Kara's Flowers were ready to sign on the dotted line. "Reprise liked what they heard and went after them," John told the author. "Our lawyer had not yet completed our contract and unfortunately for Omad Productions, we lost out to the big record label."

Reprise paid a compensation fee and offered what they described as "a two-point override" on the next two albums – but it didn't quite swallow Tommy's disappointment. It had been an equally difficult decision for Kara's Flowers, but – after some initial reluctance – it was time for them to start afresh with Reprise.

3

Boulevard Of Broken Dreams

KARA's Flowers were finally signed. As they were about to learn, however, the hard work was far from over.

"[Some] bands go, 'Oh, we're on Reprise now, so that means people are going to like us. You're going to get our record played on the radio because we're on Reprise,'" Rob Cavallo sighed. "Well, no. That doesn't work at all. No matter what we do or how much money we spend, there's no such thing as a 'made' hit any more. Kids have to respond. The goal is not to get signed – the goal is to do great music."

The pressure was on. The quartet still had everything to prove. Throughout 1996 they threw themselves into songwriting, trying desperately to produce material that justified the faith Rob had in them.

"They were being marketed as the next Green Day with a twist," one of their friends told the author, "but their previous songwriting sessions weren't enough. Reprise wanted to stretch them a bit further and see what they were capable of."

All eyes were on them, but the high expectations and the feeling that their success was not 'made' as they thought, but solely dependent on the quality of the future work proved cripplingly inhibiting. According to friends, Adam had his biggest flashes of creative brilliance when he was totally unselfconscious, but those days were gone – with the spotlight focused on him, like a rabbit caught in headlights he would retreat from the glare. The close scrutiny would prove an invaluable grounding for the showbiz world they would later inhabit; back then though, it just felt as though they were being tested. As the group's primary songwriter, Adam began to flash back to his earlier moments of awkwardness, when he would perform entire shows with his back to the audience. He was plagued with self-doubt and those dark feelings manifested themselves in the material.

'Good Evening Dr Nothing', for instance, referred to having won a war – a metaphor for finally fighting his way to a record deal – but not knowing what now lay in store. As Adam now knew all too well, signing with Reprise was just the beginning. Taking on the character of a faded Hollywood starlet, he also stepped forward in time to envisage himself as someone bestowed with the blessing of fame who also had a "hole in his soul".

'The Powers That Be', meanwhile, spoke of the frustrating impotence of pre-fame anonymity. It told of days wasted in the rain or spent waiting fruitlessly by the phone. If it had been any other day, Adam vowed, he would rebel and "wrestle [with the] powers that be", but he is held back by the inescapable truth that he lacks bargaining power as an unknown.

'Grave Condition' spoke of a lonely voyage of self-discovery. Yet the mood lifted, telling of when he encountered by chance an extraordinary woman in the forecourt of a local petrol station – and she captured his heart.

The crush was a counter-intuitive one – at that time, like many boys his age, Adam was infatuated with tanned, blonde and buxom stars such as Pamela Anderson, and this mystery woman was nothing like the *Penthouse* fantasy images that adorned his bedroom walls. In stark contrast to the artificial glamour for which LA was famed, this girl had shorter than average dark hair, a porcelain complexion and only very subtle curves. With no highlights or extensions, no fake tan or cosmetic augmentation – in a city saturated by archetypal Californian blondes, she stood out like a sore thumb. In spite of – or perhaps even because of – her deviation from conventional beauty, she was instantly appealing to Adam. Mysterious and edgy, she was giving nothing away – and the more aloof and elusive she appeared, the more Adam lusted after her.

He wrote the song 'Angel In Blue Jeans' about the moment he first saw her – someone he felt had "melted" all his bitterness away. The lyrics read like a historical reference book of chat-up lines, talking of an angel who would be the first to fly to heaven, someone with "moonbeams in her eyes" who he knows as well as he knows the sun. When he didn't know so much as her name, Adam questioned, how could he miss her already? Whether it seemed touching and romantic or horribly clichéd and – uncharacteristically for a teenage Adam – saccharine and soppy depended on the listener's perspective, but in any case it described the moment he fell in love at first sight.

The experience added authenticity to Adam's writing – now he was no longer calculating the perfect formula for a punk-pop song, but writing organically from the heart. The melodies flowed more naturally now. 'Come Talk With Me' was a track about the same encounter, allowing him to ask all that he hadn't dared to at the petrol station – why wouldn't she talk to him?

Regardless of this, she had cured his lyrical awkwardness and writer's block. When he finally found out her name, he wrote 'My Ocean Blue' in her honour. Portraying her as an awe-inspiring woman of sufficient strength to sink the *Titanic*, he sang of his "darling Jane". The mystery had been solved – the petrol station siren was Jane Herman, a writer in the making with a passion for fashion who, years later, would become the editor of *Vogue*.

Lusting after someone who seemed at first to be unattainable, Adam gently and gradually broke down her defences, persuading her to go on a date with him. That was just the beginning – she would provide plenty more songwriting inspiration in the years to come.

Within weeks of Adam's first date with Jane, the time had come to narrow down the material for Kara's Flowers' official album. The tracks from his period of depression, such as 'Grave Condition', 'The Powers That Be' and 'Good Evening Dr Nothing', were among the first to be sacrificed. 'My Ocean Blue' was declared album material, while the earlier tracks about Jane were not. However, every song they recorded with John DeNicola and Tommy Allan was carried over to the album, with the exception of 'Ray Pim' and 'Revenge Of The Kill Toys'. The aim of extracting these was to hone a more mature sound. Finally, with the addition of bonus track 'Buddy Two Shoes Wilson', the track-list was complete.

Now all the group needed for their album was a title. After a little deliberation, they chose *The Fourth World* – based on their fantasy of becoming rock gods, it was a highly ambitious reference to a fictional universe in which they would be portrayed that way.

"The name was inspired by [1994 film] *Heavenly Creatures*," one of the band's friends explained to the author. "It was a sort of science fiction concept of an alternative universe – a heaven where the religion isn't

Christianity or any kind of god, but where musicians and creative people are worshipped as saints instead."

Indeed, in the Fourth World, music was the modern day Bible – and those who practised it were revered. It was a place where the only restriction on their dreams was the limits of their imagination – and Kara's Flowers were not lacking in that.

The film from which the name was derived centres around the obsessive relationship between two young – and possibly lesbian – women at a time when Sapphic love was regarded as a psychological aberration. The film was based on a real-life case in fifties New Zealand, with some of its voiceovers comprising the character Pauline Parker's actual diary entries.

The two girls, Pauline (Melanie Lynskey) and Juliet (Kate Winslet), originally bond over a childhood history of ill health and soon become inseparable, much to the concern of their parents, who fear there is a romantic element. Over time the friendship becomes ever more intense and all-consuming and when it emerges that Juliet must move to South Africa, both become increasingly hysterical. They soon hatch a plot to murder Pauline's mother, bludgeoning her over the head with a brick in a quiet park. While the two had hoped to run away together to the USA, sharing a common goal of becoming playwrights, the murder – along with diary entries planning it – is soon discovered, culminating in a lengthy jail sentence for both.

Throughout the film, various distressing scenes unfold involving ill health, family hostility and the prospect of the girls' separation from each other – and that is when the Fourth World comes into play. A fantasy concept invented by Juliet as a coping mechanism, it detaches the girls from reality, offering them an escape to a place where no one and nothing can harm them. The Fourth World is meaningful because it is rich in the freedom that both lack at home.

Of course, what appealed to the band was that musicians and artists were celebrated and revered in that world. Helping them on their way towards living that dream of superstar status was Rob Cavallo, who combined his production with mixing by renowned punk rock engineer Jerry Finn. Like Rob, Jerry had formerly worked on *Dookie*, as well as Green Day's subsequent 1995 follow-up, *Insomniac*. His back catalogue also included tracks for Pennywise and Rancid, while – in the years leading up to his

2008 death from a heart attack and brain haemorrhage – he would also make a name for himself with Alkaline Trio, the Offspring, Sum 41 and Blink 182. This sound was exactly the direction Reprise envisaged for Kara's Flowers – accessible punk pop with guitars.

Fittingly, Finn would pile layer upon layer of rock sound to the tracks while combining the genre he knew best with beats that suited the group's additional sixties pop twist. While there were sprinklings of the on-trend Green Day sound, it was blended with added extras such as the tender ballad vibe of 'To Her With Love'. 'My Ocean Blue' was the closest track on the album to the sound that would later be adopted by Maroon 5 – unabashed pop.

After the drums were cut, engineer Ken Allardyce was drafted in to work on the overdubs, having been simultaneously developing Green Day's *Nimrod*. "My first impressions were of four fresh-faced and enthusiastic kids who seemed very confident with their catchy hooks," he told the author. "They were not at all overawed with the situation. They were quite British-sounding with their pop tunes albeit with a healthy dose of loud guitars. [They didn't] quite sound like anyone else [but] the Fab Four were definitely lurking in the background! I'm not sure how one would categorise it, but alt progressive pop would cover it for me!"

Ken quickly singled out Adam as the driving force behind that sound. "Their greatest strength was undoubtedly his voice," he said. "He was a complete natural talent." In addition, he possessed charismatic leadership qualities and an addiction to being the centre of attention – the only downside being that Ken struggled to comprehend the group's often random and at times unintelligible lyrics.

Aside from a hiccup when a track they'd been working on was "erased by an overzealous assistant", the studio sessions progressed well – although Allardyce became a little frustrated when, due to the pressures of juggling the beginnings of a career with school, their work together was regularly interrupted.

"Those early days were a bit chaotic," he observed, "as these guys were still school-kids. They would arrive at the studio from school mid-afternoon and have to be at home and in bed ready for school the next day, so they were out of the studio again pretty early. This, as well as assorted absenteeisms for play practice, etc, made for a pretty disjointed recording schedule. We recorded the tracks when we could, but I do remember thinking we could have benefited from more continuity and fewer distractions."

That aspect aside, the band's maturity, steely focus and "versatile musicianship" might have led him to forget that he was dealing with teenagers. But while Ken was frustrated that progress had stalled, Adam was enjoying the privileges that his rock-star-in-the-making status afforded.

"I was doing really badly," he would mischievously acknowledge, "because I was spending my time writing music instead of doing home-work – [but] I miraculously graduated because I could say, 'Sorry, I didn't do that paper because I was in the studio!'"

Concessions made for him meant that he could skip work from time to time and earn grades based on his yearly average thus far, instead of pains-takingly completing every single essay. Meanwhile, Adam soaked up the attention from curious teachers and star-struck classmates alike, boasting of how his album's production credits read just like those of his A-list idols. At the same time, those bandmates with more retiring personalities – such as Jesse – were slightly embarrassed by their newfound fame and the atten-tion it elicited. But when graduation day came, there was a collective feeling of relief. With the inconvenience of school finally behind them, the group threw themselves wholeheartedly into promoting the album.

Their schedule kicked off with a performance on an episode of popular TV show *Beverley Hills 90210*. "I had been obsessed with that show," Adam recalled fondly to *The Advocate*. "Any young boy knew that in order to start talking to girls, you needed to be into 90210. So we went on the show and [actress] Tiffani-Amber Thiessen thought we were all on blow. We were just excited! She said, 'You guys are partying, right?' We're like, 'We're 17, Tiffani-Amber Thiessen – what are you talking about?'"

Of course, in the USA, even entry to a nightclub was strictly forbidden before the age of 21 – and according to Adam, none of the band members had taken their chances with fake ID. High on adrenalin alone, he added: "Tori Spelling hung out with us backstage and gave us the lowdown. Brian Austin Green kept telling us about his music. Ian Ziering was kind of a dick. Maybe he was having a bad day!"

Following the TV show, 'Soap Disco' was selected as the first single and released on July 22, 1997. Its B-side was the early version of 'Captain Splendid' that the group had recorded with John and Tommy. The album closely followed on August 19.

Meanwhile, Ryan – whose plan B if the band flopped was to become a Democratic politician – was still studying English Literature at local university UCLA. He was deliberating over whether to drop out and focus full-time on the band but had been holding back, reluctant to commit until Kara's Flowers became a demonstrable success.

Live shows were a good way of testing the water. Sure enough, the group were soon invited out on the road to support artists such as Reel Big Fish, Aquabats, Goldfinger and Save Ferris. "For some reason, ska bands really like us," Adam observed, adding with a characteristic lack of diplomacy, "even though we're not really a ska band."

Unfortunately, as Aaron Barrett of Reel Big Fish recalled, sometimes they were also subjected to downright hostility. Aaron's first experience of the group dated back to almost two years earlier, when he'd seen Kara's Flowers support a virtually unknown act in a small club in LA. Initially, his expectations hadn't been high.

"Some friends had forced me against my will to go see a band called That Dog," he told the author, "who I really didn't like at all. The place was pretty empty when the first band of the night walked up; they were these young teenage looking boys all in mod-ish three-button suits. We all looked at each other and joked about how they looked just like the band from the recent movie *That Thing You Do* – that or a ska band. Then they started to play and we were all blown away. I couldn't believe how amazing these guys sounded, they were all such talented musicians and Adam's voice was incredible, even way back then. This is before he started singing like Stevie Wonder and sang more like a sweet, precious, baby Paul Simon. There was a big Beatles influence but also this dreamy power-pop sound that I had never heard anything like in my life. I just couldn't get over how good it was. I think they became my favourite band of all time right then and there."

In fact, Aaron liked them so much that he persuaded his manager to book them as the support act at Reel Big Fish's very next show. Already ambivalent about what he perceived as the "weak" band name, Adam then elected to change it for that concert, held at the Showcase Theatre in

Corona, California. That night – and for one night only – they appeared onstage as The Roundabouts.

Fast forward to late 1997. Reel Big Fish were taking the band out on the road again, but this time for a full-length tour. However the experience was a humiliating one – ill-suited to their audience, they were hit by a barrage of abuse.

"It was very rough for them," Aaron continues, "because it was 1997 and the height of the nineties ska craze. Even though they always sounded great and played so well, they got booed through just about every song, just about every night. I used to watch them play every night and get so mad at our fans for being so mean to them. But now, looking back, I'm not sure what we were expecting. People had come to see a ska show and they definitely didn't want to hear the kind of music that Kara's Flowers played. We were just big music lovers and we liked all kinds of music and we were hoping that our fans would give them a chance but it just wasn't the right time for such an eclectic band to be on the bill. I just wanted to get this amazing band out playing in front of a lot of people but it was just the wrong audience."

It didn't help that Kara's Flowers would often end shows with a rendition of 'Baba O' Riley' by the Who, a track which served to confuse the crowd all the more. One night, however, during a disastrous show in Tulsa, Oklahoma, an exasperated Aaron decided to prove a point to his fans.

"Kara's Flowers had a particularly rough night," he recalls, "people booing and throwing things their whole set. They even cut a few songs just to get offstage! Well, I was just so pissed that these mean ska fans had practically booed my favourite band off the stage and I was still stewing about it halfway through our set so our band launched into a straight (not ska, just exactly like the album) version of a Kara's Flowers song. I think it was 'Loving The Small Time', and the audience went CRAZY; dancing, jumping, moshing, the works. Then at the end I said, 'Thank you, that song was by our opening band tonight, Kara's Flowers . . . who you guys all booed off the stage.' I don't know what point it really proved but it was an interesting moment."

Fortunately the group fared better on some of their other early tours. For Nate Bott of the Siren Six, their failure to fit the ska mould didn't matter in the slightest.

"We had a similar mod fashion sense and a pop sensibility and attitude," he told the author. "The ones who swayed a little more punk and indie were into us and the mainstream pop fans attached themselves to Kara's Flowers. But really we're all in the same room together and differences that seemed so drastic then are more like different pairs of pants these days! They all loved the Beatles and Britpop and that was good enough for me – although that 'Teddy Ruxpin is a whore' line always puzzled me a bit!"

Nate and his bandmates had first met Kara's Flowers on January 2, 1998 – the very first day they moved to LA. Just before they'd left their home city of Minneapolis, a friend had passed a copy of *The Fourth World* on to them – and it had stopped them in their tracks. "I remember we were all impressed that it had been produced by Rob Cavallo," Nate recalled, "because Green Day had just broken pretty huge."

That night, both bands met at a Jerry's Deli to discuss the possibility of a joint tour – and bonded over a mutual loathing for rock-rappers Limp Bizkit. "I remember them being extremely welcoming, highly intelligent and hilarious people," Nate continued. "There was definitely a strong mod vibe going on. We were all very sensitive young people trying to form our identities . . . At the time Limp Bizkit was the cat's meow, so we were bonded by common enemies as well."

Both groups had released an album within a month of each other; although the Siren Six had a slight head-start with a previous album in 1994, under the less than flattering moniker Stinkfish, both were still finding their feet. Consequently they shared the same feverish excitement at winning over audiences for the first time.

"Touring with Kara's Flowers was a blast," recalled Nate. "We got to see them just as they were breaking through, selling out 800–1,000 capacity clubs. Those kinds of shows are pretty magical. Equal levels of excitement from the band and audience. The bands' are excited that their sound is working and the audience is excited that their band is getting big. It was a first-hand example of how it used to happen for bands before the music industry crashed.

"We were competitive," he added, "but there was always a mutual respect for one another because we knew we were taking very different approaches. We pushed each other to do better and we supported each other. The shows were always filled with youthful exuberance and the feeling that we were really exerting ourselves, that it was possible to change things."

Indeed, Kara's Flowers were intent on unleashing a new hybrid of blue-grass, contemporary and vintage pop, punk and old-fashioned rock'n'roll on the world – and 1998 looked like it might be the year they succeeded. That year also saw them showcase a track which had narrowly missed a spot on the album – 'Yesterday When I Was Handsome', a retrospective ballad about the pain of loss which shared similarities with the Beatles' 'Yesterday'. As with his older counterpart, Paul McCartney, Adam's lyric was also influenced by his relationship with a girlfriend named Jane. (In McCartney's case it had been actress Jane Asher.)

The track formed part of *Hear You Me: A Tribute To Mykel And Carli*, an album put together by Weezer to pay their respects to two deceased sisters who'd attended dozens of their shows. They'd described themselves as 'super groupies' albeit without the sexual connotations sometimes attached to the tag. Years earlier, they'd befriended Weezer while they were still struggling to get on the ladder and the band had written the track 'Mykel And Carli' in appreciation. Soon after, the girls agreed to run their official fan club, combining this work with regular appearances at the concerts. When they were tragically killed in a car accident en route to a show – there was later speculation that one of the girls had fallen asleep at the wheel – Weezer released the tribute album to pay their respects. Proceeds were offered to the sisters' family to help with funeral costs.

However, while the compilation album – which saw Kara's Flowers share the bill with scores of other up and coming artists – was a success, the same couldn't have been said for Kara's Flowers' own album release. One reviewer had predicted, "*The Fourth World* will be rammed down your throat for months . . . it's the sort of joyously delivered [music] that bores its way into your skull after only one listen – and it'll be huge." The reality, however, was enormously different.

The reviews they received from niche fanzines and small music websites were overwhelmingly negative, whereas most of the big hitters – the likes of VH1 and MTV – deemed them scarcely important enough to scrape a negative mention. While some small scale websites dismissed their music as "disgustingly insipid", claiming it featured "some of the worst lyrics ever to find their way into Western pop music", when it came to the outlets they truly wanted to target, the silence was deafening. Without the support – or attention – of major media sources, the album seemed doomed.

Yet the critics' choice didn't always match that of the public. In later years, Lady Gaga, Amy Winehouse and Katy Perry would all endure the acid tongue of the press, receiving eye-wateringly caustic one-out-of-10-star reviews, only to raise a middle finger in the faces of their detractors by selling millions of copies of the same songs they'd dismissed.

For an earlier example of this, Kara's Flowers needed look no further than Green Day. With enormous irony, while *Dookie* had quickly been certified multi-platinum, one of a number of bad reviews had declared it "self-congratulatory garbage that had 'utterly failed'". The contrast between the review and the reality was telling. While the critics might tout themselves as experts, a professional opinion clearly counted for nothing when it came to predicting the passions of the public. In any case – fortunately for Kara's Flowers – in the days before Google, a negative history was easy to erase.

As for the problem of being ignored by many media sources altogether, they could again look to Green Day for validation. Their first two albums hadn't registered on any chart, but that hadn't stopped them excelling thereafter. Reviewers' opinions – or a total lack thereof – were not the be all and end all. In the end, only the listeners would decide.

Yet, dishearteningly for the group, even establishing a small fanbase would initially prove challenging. Despite this, Adam was clearly enjoying living up to every rock'n'roll cliché – according to Nate of the Siren Six, he'd even accumulated an army of groupies.

"The very first time I ever saw Adam, he was getting out of a rented limo with a girl around each arm," he told the author. "He was good at playing the rock star."

However, the fantasy didn't yet match the reality, as their disastrous early shows would demonstrate. "We played this bar in a small town in Oregon," Adam recalled for *Blender*, "and there was nobody there. Halfway through our set the bartender left, so there was literally not one person in the building. We finished our set and put our things in the van and cried ourselves to sleep."

The biggest reality check of all was yet to come – far from the chart success their label had expected, *The Fourth World* scarcely sold a thousand copies. Despite a hefty cash injection for promotion and a tour that had taken them across America, it just hadn't caught fire. As Rob Cavallo had noted, signing with a major label alone was never enough to guarantee success – it was all down to the unpredictable nature of the public.

As Kara's Flowers trailed from one uninterested audience to another, determined to finish the tour, group morale was at an all-time low. The burning question was: what had gone wrong?

There were numerous issues. Firstly, there was Reprise's decision to send them on the road with a succession of ska bands. Often the only group outside of that genre on a crowded bill, they were an easy target for the public's drunken derision. While Mickey had idealistically described some of these musical culture clashes as "compatible", where punters came purely to "dance and have fun and jump up and down and like happy music", no matter what its sound, at others they'd been heckled relentlessly – or, worse still, completely ignored. "There are always the few purists who are very closed minded," Mickey said at the time, "who tell us we'd be better if we had horns – but it's fine."

It clearly wasn't. It didn't help that their label had the most experience with (and the most interest in) punk groups. This was the genre that predominated at Reprise, whereas Kara's Flowers' sound was continually evolving. They still had a passion for Green Day and Weezer, but musically they were branching out – and playing to purely punk/ska audiences was scarcely helping to widen their appeal.

Yet at that time, the popularity of ska overshadowed acts like theirs and they struggled to achieve adequate radio play. "[Radio] is very afraid to play anything out of its format," Mickey had groaned, "and right now they're stuck in their ways. Things seem to be getting more poppy and more happy which is good, but at this point if it's not electronic or if it's not ska, it's like it's kind of hard to get on there . . . it's hard for a baby band to get airplay."

Breaking America was in itself an enormous challenge, regardless of whether the band could secure ample airplay. Unlike Britain, where large national stations such as Radio 1 predominate, the vast size of the USA meant there wasn't one single channel through which Kara's Flowers could court success. To make their mark, they faced an expensive, exhausting and time-consuming road trip to win over every single region one by one. To truly achieve a national profile, they'd have to personally visit and perform for hundreds of radio stations – but, due to the frosty reception the album had received, it was one financial commitment too many for Reprise. Besides, it was also too much for four teenage boys who were just out of school – not least for Ryan, who had to juggle touring commitments with a college degree. A consensus was building that the group just wasn't ready.

While radio stations and music fans alike were often reluctant to step outside their genre of choice, there was another factor that divided Kara's Flowers from their target audience: their age. At face value, it was a novelty – how many other teenagers in the adult-oriented music industry of the nineties would be performing in large nightclubs? Yet while it initially got them noticed, they struggled to be taken seriously for exactly the same reason. Their typical fans were not starry-eyed preteens with dreams of marrying a pop pin-up – in fact, at the shows Reprise had booked them for, the audiences were almost invariably older and tougher.

"You had these baby-faced teenage boys playing to macho, meathead punk guys with mohawks, drinking cans of lager and swearing at them," one onlooker recalled incredulously. Needless to say, it wasn't a match and their 'cute' power-pop tunes didn't translate. Above all, their appearance meant they were often stereotyped and automatically written off as unsuitable for serious indie-rock fans.

The lyricism was another giveaway of their age – music fans in their twenties and thirties would recoil in embarrassment from phrases that sounded as though they belonged to children's action movies. Kara's Flowers were overthrowing killer slime and escaping the clutches of teddy bears – it was different but, again, it didn't cut it with lovers of punk or ska, or with older rock fans in general.

At the other extreme, American audiences were also very discerning and ultra-critical about the appearance of their pop icons. While the boys were attractive, they hadn't yet grown into their looks. Back then they were nerdy, floppy-haired and unpolished – and that alone put their appeal with hormonal young girls into question. Many were attracted instead to the more obvious charms of "pretty" boy bands like N-Sync and Backstreet Boys.

Yet did looks truly matter when it came to music? One magazine article hit the nail on the head about the perils of giving appearances preferential treatment when it came to chooing talent with the telling headline: "*Ask Men* Readers Rank 99 Most Desirable Women In Music And Inadvertently Create World's Worst Play List".

This superficial aspect within music wasn't limited to male tastes either, as male pop bands could usually be neatly categorised into one of two groups. There were the boys with toned six-packs and polished-to-perfection faces, who made TV shows and magazine covers, and then there were those who had faces rather cruelly reserved for radio – those who, in spite of obvious talent, might never make it to mainstream. At this early stage in their development, Kara's Flowers belonged to the latter.

While it was nothing that a haircut and an image makeover wouldn't have easily solved, there were also commitment issues. Unfortunately, failing to ingratiate themselves with regional radio stations had made a negative impact.

"Kara's Flowers was just floating up the wall beneath the sticks," Adam would later tell *Pure Songwriters*. "Make a record quickly, put it out. No touring base, no nothing. Just try to make it happen right out of the gate and it just doesn't work. Even if it was to work, it still doesn't, because you may become famous or successful or sell a million records or win a Grammy, but it will all die away so quickly. I just feel like, to have longevity, you gotta earn it. You gotta have a base. You gotta kind of suffer a little bit. Tour as a band for a year and do all of the shit that rock bands are supposed to do in order to achieve it. Otherwise it's kind of this weird, flimsy, soulless fame that goes away really quickly."

Wise words, but ones that Adam ultimately struggled to live up to himself. At one scheduled concert, he hadn't even shown up.

"We played the music," Jesse cringed, "and had people in the audience come up onstage and sing karaoke versions of our songs." When he was later asked why he hadn't arrived that night, he'd shrugged his shoulders nonchalantly and retorted, "Didn't feel like it."

"It angers me so much to hear you admit that," Ryan went on record as saying. "You were like a freaking child playing sick to get out of school."

Yet underneath the cool exterior lurked the real reason for a no-show – a lack of self-esteem. Adam had suffered from stage fright and, motivated by a fear of burning out and losing his voice for an important upcoming showcase, he'd decided to save himself for it. Unfortunately, that had meant disappointing an audience – and destroying an already fragile reputation that they were not famous enough to adequately repair.

Of course, Adam could have delivered a gushing apology for his misdemeanours (*à la* Justin Bieber in more recent times), but, without an established fanbase to hear it, every word would be redundant. Those who'd just been introduced to the band wouldn't be taking second chances – they'd merely write them off as a joke act not worth investing their time and money in.

Adam had been immature and, like his bandmates, overwhelmed by the challenges of touring. On one level he believed the hype in the press releases, but beneath the surface, there remained a deep-rooted uncertainty – a fear of failure – that was driving his more erratic behaviour. Of course, his fear became a self-fulfilling prophecy and Adam was forced to watch his dreams fall down.

"They pumped us with so much crap," he told *Billboard* later. "Like, 'You guys are going to be huge. Here's some money.' We were like, 'OK, cool. Eighteen, sweet. No college, kick ass.' We did it and failed – it was a rude awakening. It really humbled us very quickly."

Of course, the group's tender age meant that they hadn't truly found themselves – personally or musically. Rob Cavallo was adamant in stating, "The great artists ALWAYS have an artistic vision as to how they are going to present themselves."

Yet that wasn't the case with Kara's Flowers. Their influences came from far and wide and the only central overriding theme was a love of the Beatles.

"We were so different as a power pop band," Jesse would later lament. "We were huge Beatles fans, but I don't think we mastered their sense of taste at all. We were 17-year-old Beatles maniacs, running around the studio with our heads cut off like chickens, saying, 'Let's have an orchestra come in here!'"

Meanwhile John DeNicola felt that they never fully recaptured the raw grassroots energy of their first recordings with him. "They took a long time to re-record the same songs," he opined of the Reprise album, "and spent 10 times as much as we did. The resulting record was, in my biased opinion, less fresh and immediate-sounding than ours. Sometimes it's hard to re-record a song and capture that same immediacy and fire as the first recording – and for Kara's Flowers, that moment was lost."

Sound engineer Ken Allardyce echoed the band's own dissatisfaction with the quality of the early material. "It was a good but not great album," he reflected. "I think it lacked the universal appeal of a breakthrough record because, as with the demo sessions, they had not yet fully defined their sound and the piecemeal way it was put together is somewhat reflected in the result."

Due to the unexpected failure of the album – something none of the famed taste-makers at Reprise could have predicted – support was dwindling for the group. Things were about to get even worse when it emerged that Rob Cavallo, their main cheerleader at the label and the man who'd originally signed them, was leaving.

He'd been the only one they'd felt was truly on their side. Without Cavallo around, they were left to ponder his words about exactly what made an album fail. "If you could buy a radio station and say, 'You will play this record,'" he'd told them, "and let's say they play it three times a day for two weeks. If that record doesn't respond, if the kids aren't buying it, if the kids don't call in and say they really like it, you're not going to have a hit – no matter what. The only thing that brings kids and music fans into the stores to actually buy a record is that they're interested in what the band is saying and doing and playing."

It was a painful realisation for the group who, up until that point, might have thought getting signed to Reprise was a means to an end within itself. The fact remained that, regardless of what they did, it all came down to that mysterious chemistry between a band and their public – either it was there or it wasn't.

"When you're 17, you're in high school, you're cocky and you have people telling you you're gonna be huge, you're like, 'Sweet. Cool. We're going to be famous. Our problems are going to be solved,'" Adam later recalled. "By Christmas we were going to be famous. What happened was that by Christmas, our record was in the garbage can."

"We were discouraged because we had extremely high hopes and we were young and we were on top of the world," Mickey added. "Then everything fell through."

The foursome already felt desperately low and the loss of Rob Cavallo was the final straw. Now they had only strangers for company at the label, none of whom they felt cared enough to keep their best interests at heart. As a bitter Ryan would explain, "Somebody once told me that nobody is ever going to love or work as hard for, or support our band as much as we are. No-one's going to love what you do and stand behind you 'til the end as much as you are. The struggle is to find people who feel like it's their project almost as much as it is yours."

With this in mind, the boys realised they had become increasingly dis-illusioned with manager Pat Magnarella. Pat was Rob's right-hand man and the two often worked in collaboration. The pair had worked with each other on Green Day and had even guided Weezer's debut, *The Blue Album*, to triple platinum success together. He had been described in a press release as "a visionary manager with a solid track record for nurtur-ing long-term careers" – but Kara's Flowers no longer agreed with that.

In fact, Mickey even inferred that they felt they'd been viewed as pawns to be manipulated for financial gain, lamenting to *Star Polish*, "That [a manager or label] loves your music is ultimately the most important thing. If someone looks at you merely as a commodity, then they will not be suc-cessful in terms of longevity of your career."

The boys decided to part ways with Pat – and simultaneously asked to be released from their contract with Reprise, leaving them free to start anew. So what next? Success had consistently eluded them, but in any case, by Adam's own admission, "We definitely weren't ready."

As teenagers, criticism as harsh as they'd received felt lethal – and there'd been nothing to prepare them for it. Those in charge of their career had perpetually massaged their egos, lulling them into a false sense of security and making them all the more vulnerable to failure. Unsurpris-ingly, playing to almost empty auditoriums had hit hard. When a crowd did show, the boos and catcalls were at times so loud that they couldn't even be drowned out by the music.

Then there were the negative reviews, the words of which seemed to burn indelibly into Adam's brain. According to reviewers such as a critic from *Meanstreet*, his ballads were "disgustingly insipid", his lyrics nonsensi-cal and the album was the worst music to hit the stores that decade. Much of the scorn centred on Adam as the lead singer and songwriter – and it was far too heavy a burden to bear for someone so young.

At this particular moment there was a serious question mark over whether to even carry on. "It was difficult to stay together," Adam mused to *RAD* magazine. "It's like you don't know what you are going to do with your life, even though you seem to be on a path – so we got kind of discouraged and we didn't know if we would stay together. There was a lot of indecision."

One thing was for sure: if they were to stand any chance of succeeding, they'd need to change their formula. Anxious to reinvent themselves, Jesse and Adam broke away from their bandmates and, in September 1998, started musical tuition classes at Five Towns College – a small liberal arts school in Dix Hills, Long Island, New York.

To say that it was a change of scenery was an understatement. The rugged, multicultural New York City suburbs of Long Island were a million miles away from the wealthy, glamorous, almost sanitised vibe of everyday life in upscale California. While Dix Hills was an affluent neighbourhood, it bordered Wyandanch – a poverty-stricken ghetto. In an 85 per cent black neighbourhood, one in five of Wyandanch's residents were living below the poverty line. It was the type of area that would inflame the sympathies of Adam's politically driven uncle. An award-winning, almost exclusively white school lay a mere couple of miles away from a desperately failing, predominantly black one – sharp evidence of the racial divide.

The main strip in the area, Straight Path, was home to rows of long since abandoned, empty storefronts with decades-old paint peeling from their outer walls. The only sign of life came from the tatty market stalls, all offering cheap, mass-produced, ethnically styled clothes. At the time Adam and Jesse arrived, some charity initiatives were trying desperately to inject hope into the area – but largely without success.

Yet just as the blues had grown out of the griot tradition under the harsh conditions of slavery, the hardship in Wyandanch was a motivating factor for creativity too. The tougher life was, the more deprived and anguished the ghetto residents felt, the more they had a compulsion to pour their pain into music. As Adam later commented, "I think pain is the best feeling for songwriting" – and with that statement, he hit precisely upon the very essence and life blood of soul music: something that flowed through the veins of his new Long Island home.

"You can write good, happy songs," added Adam, "but the kind of depressing ones are more effective. Songs are easier to write when impassioned and angry. It's a good way to channel that negative energy."

It was well-timed, of course, that on his arrival at Dix Hills, he would be introduced to this musical genre almost as a form of therapy – one he hadn't previously known existed. "All I knew when I was younger was Paul McCartney and Paul Simon," a shamefaced Adam confessed to the *Philadelphia Enquirer*. "Listening to Stevie Wonder changed everything."

"I think there's a stigma attached to Stevie Wonder," he added, "as far as him being the guy that wrote 'I Just Called To Say I Love You'. Being a child of the eighties, that's all I had really thought of him. I didn't really know he had all these classic records and when I started listening to songs like 'Sir Duke', 'I Wish' and 'I Believe', it really just changed my whole life as a singer, songwriter and musician."

Of course, it wasn't only the music of that legendary son of Detroit that inspired him during his time on Long Island. Embracing a period he would describe as his "reawakening", Adam and Jesse opened their eyes to a culture that was alien – yet increasingly attractive – to them.

"We were staying in a predominantly black dormitory," Adam told *RAD* of his experience, "and we were the minority. It was such a different community. We would wake up in the morning and there would be gospel blasting and hip-hop and stuff that one had never really been exposed to. I really fell in love with it."

Another artist who moved him was Jay-Z, who had recently risen from underground status to become a mainstream hip-hop artist. Ironically, this was exactly where Kara's Flowers then stood – they were at a crossroads, but ready to make a musical change.

"I remember when I first heard 'Hard Knock Life'," Adam told *RAD* with barely concealed admiration. "I was like, 'Damn! That is revolutionary shit!'"

Not only was the sound new to him, but he noted that the rapper was using his soapbox to make a political statement about inequality, caustically depicting what life was like for a black person from a deprived neighbourhood. The use of children in the accompanying video drove the point home even further – they were suffering and had barely been given a chance in life.

The irony was that affluent white listeners would buy into the track in their droves, putting Jay-Z on the international map and making him millions. Jay-Z was from a deprived New York neighbourhood himself and the very people he might have symbolically regarded as his oppressors would inadvertently help create his wealth. Unlike some of his material, which featured scores of references to 'hos' and 'bitches' that many would find offensively sexist, this track was hard-hitting and intended to make a political impact.

Adam relished the combination of big beats and candid emotion. Each morning, he began to look forward to the diversity of sound that would pour out from every hallway. His tastes soon expanded to include Fugees Lauryn Hill and Wyclef Jean – the latter of whom attended Five Towns himself years earlier – along with those other sometime collaborators Missy Elliott and Timbaland – in the days before the latter broke into the mainstream – and veteran Bill Withers, whose most famous hit, 'Ain't No Sunshine', had been released in 1971.

It couldn't have come at a better time. "I was born and raised listening to Simon & Garfunkel and the Beatles and stuff," Adam recalled, "which was really good for songwriting, but I felt I needed to look elsewhere for vocal inspiration."

What was more, he began to feel that genres like soul were better suited to his voice than the rock music that had been an obvious choice back home in LA. "I was like, 'I can sing like that!'" he recalled jubilantly, "and I started to really love soul music."

As Mickey would playfully describe, he and Jesse spent that unforgettable semester "driving cross-country at a breakneck pace" and "coming up with colourful names for our classmates"!

"We had friends named Chaos and shit," Adam would confirm to MTV. "It was NOT Brentwood High!"

In fact, their commitment to soaking up black music and culture was such a priority that Adam had ended up flunking his classes. "I failed guitar," he would admit shamefacedly, "which is really sad. It's mostly because I didn't show up. I actually went towards the end and said, 'What can I do to make it up?' and the teacher said, 'Don't worry about it, man!' – he was all hippied out – 'You're fine.' Then he put an F on my transcript. I'll never forget him."

Jesse had fared a little better with his piano lessons, revisiting the beloved instrument for the first time since early childhood – but the priority was not to follow the curriculum religiously to get a qualification. Rather, they hoped to learn things that couldn't be taught, that were far more valuable than a certificate on a sheet of paper. They were looking for a fresh perspective on life and music – something that would save and rejuvenate Kara's Flowers.

Thanks to Five Towns, their horizons really did expand – over time, they'd move away from their teenage rebellion rock phase. They were no longer pseudo-angst-ridden teenagers copying Green Day, or – as their detractors might cynically describe it – privileged rich kids faking those emotions to be perceived as cool.

"Growing up was gradual because we've been together for so long," Adam later explained to the *Mirror*. "At 14 or 15, we were into the Green Days and the Weezers of the world. Eventually [when] we stumbled on soul and R&B, I really latched onto it and felt passionate about it in a way I hadn't felt about anything since my youth . . . it was nice to have a reawakening."

It had taken this time in New York to open their ears to new sonic possibilities. One of the most memorable turning points – besides playing Herbie Hancock's *Hunters* album on a loop and discovering Jay-Z – was their introduction to 'Are You That Somebody?', a collaboration between Aaliyah and Timbaland.

"That is one of the most revolutionary sounding songs ever recorded," Adam later told the *LA Times*. "We heard that song and we thought to ourselves, 'Whoa, there has never been anything like this before.'"

The track became an inspiration for their own sound. "We were just so sick of being a typical rock'n'roll band and doing the things a typical rock'n' roll band does," Adam explained. "So we started to latch onto that . . . I think there was a lot of audacity about that, just because of the way that we look and what kind of turned us on was we thought, 'Maybe we're doing something new!'"

Of course, that would provoke varied reactions. "I thought to myself, 'This is much more suited to me'," Adam continued. "I can sing like all these guys better than I can sing like Eddie Vedder!' We got a lot of flak for it [though]. Our loyal power-pop cool fans thought we were out of our minds."

Yet Adam and Jesse were breaking down the barriers of what was perceived as cool, shedding their LA influences and rebelling against the conventional model of rebellion. They'd always been keen to be liked by their audiences, but with time, experience and a change of scenery came a new realisation: not only was it impossible to be liked by everyone, it just didn't matter.

They were beginning to develop an enduring faith in their own musical judgment. It was all about finding the courage to follow their own instincts, without fear of alienating audiences and without any compulsion to calculate what their fanbase might prefer. Rather, they would produce their best material when they were released from the fear of how others perceived them. Realising that might just have saved Kara's Flowers.

Adam Levine makes a political statement with a T-shirt emblazoned with the word 'Feminist' while performing on the USA's *Today Show* on June 18, 2004. ERIK C PENDZICH/REX FEATURES

The band enjoys a rare moment of relaxation at the pre-Grammy Awards Party at the star-studded Beverley Hills hotel, LA on February 7, 2004. PETER BROOKER/REX FEATURES

An intimate moment is captured with Adam as he returns to one of his earliest loves: playing the drums. RETNA

James Valentine plays his part on *The Today Show* in 2004 as part of their Summer Concert Series. ERIK C PENDZICH/REX FEATURES

The band triumphantly celebrate their Best New Act win at the 2004 MTV Europe Music Awards in Rome, clutching one of their first ever trophies. BRIAN RASIC/REX FEATURES

An early moment live in concert at Las Vegas's Mandalay Bay in 2005. CHARLES SYKES/REX FEATURES

The boys show their faces at a private New York cocktail party to celebrate their success, held at the Radio City Music Hall in April 2005.
STARTRAKS PHOTO/REX FEATURES

The boys show an excessive interest in international tennis star and sex symbol Maria Sharapova after a performance at her 18th birthday party at New York's Maritime Hotel. This 2005 event would later lead to mischievous false rumours in the media that Adam had dated her and then denounced her as a "terrible lover". STARTRAKS PHOTO/REX FEATURES

Adam raises his guitar skyward during a performance at Chelmsford's V Festival in 2005. GEOFF ROBINSON/REX FEATURES

Adam lives the dream as he performs with his ultimate childhood idol, Stevie Wonder – the man he claims gave him the impetus to succeed in music – at Philadelphia's Museum of Art as part of Bob Geldof's charity event, Live 8. JOHN CHAPPLE/REX FEATURES

Jesse Carmichael rocks out during a concert series for the CBS *Early Show* in New York in September 2007 GREG ALLEN/REX FEATURES

4

There's Something About James

ADAM and Jesse returned home after just one semester – but the influence of their time at Five Towns was to last much longer. During their stint there, they'd written and recorded a nine-song CD under the name of *Four Track Demonstrations* to showcase their new sound – and when they heard it, Ryan and Mickey were transfixed.

There was the acoustic track 'If Only You Knew', which lyrically described Adam's transformation from a one-track-minded fan of punk rock and power pop to a vocalist who embraced new genres and incorporated them into his own body of work. When he sang of a beat in his heart that he didn't know what to do with, he was referring to the passion that hearing soul music for the first time had aroused in him and asking for help in channelling it.

In a second acoustic track, 'The Kid With Velvet Eyes', Adam predicts how his musical makeover will help him "survive" in a tough industry. He claims that, while there are plenty of other hopefuls out there with their "hearts on fire", he's now propelling himself to the front of the queue. The chorus warns rivals to get out of his way, insisting that he's now here to stay.

'Vanessa' is an ode to a beautiful girl that Adam knew, but doubles as a cautionary tale about the corrosive nature of the music industry and its effect on four idealistic, hopelessly naïve boys caught up in it. Embittered by his early experiences, Adam felt that the business was cut-throat and profit-orientated at the expense of embracing real artistry – something with which his bandmates would agree.

"We've learned that being signed to a major label doesn't mean you're going to be taken care of," Jesse would claim. "We are no longer naïve."

Likewise, Adam sang of a stolen innocence, lamenting that they'd come of age and been stripped of their misconceptions.

Despite that rude awakening, Adam was still holding out for his dreams, for a stroke of improbable luck that he compared to a sunrise at 3 a.m. on the song 'Shaynanni's Surprise'. (Both Adam and Jesse were friendly with Shayanni Cermeno – a fellow Californian four years their junior – and the track's title seems to be a shout-out to her.)

The pair also worked another woman into their music when, by coincidence, she called while they were in the middle of writing a song. In 'Spoke With Kate (And She Said)', Adam jokingly urges Jesse to pick up the phone but they decide to keep it ringing purely for the pleasure of hearing the mystery caller leave a message. Adam then teases that she hadn't realised what she was getting herself into when she dialled the numbers and that, as a result, will remain eternally part of the song.

Other tracks championed sheer escapism: 'Feeling Slow' fantasised about a more relaxed pace of life in the Mexican sunshine, while 'Someone More Comfortable' spoke of replacing the bullets in a gun with roses and a desire to flee from his own skin, to "slip into" someone else. The demo also featured a piano and guitar jam without lyrics that captured a similar mood.

Only 'The Sentimental Programmer' hinted at a return to the childlike science fiction fantasies of their youth. In a prime example of the 'nonsense' lyrics he was renowned for at this early stage, Adam sang of building his own robotic woman out of plastic, putting her to a "replica test" and then insisting that his creation was "iconoclastic". He would add that, although he was "crippled" with a human mind, he was actually dreaming of the android kind.

With the exception of the last song, there was very little that could be compared to Adam's earlier work. As he'd matured, his lyrical content had begun to broaden. Earlier, he'd been a wealthy boy from a privileged family, living in leafy, sheltered suburbia, with his anger and intensity possibly lacking genuine feeling. Now he had meaningful life experiences that far surpassed those of the average teenage boy – and real reasons to be angry. He'd been signed by age 17, surrounded by yes-men with their promises of near limitless success, revelled in an oh-so-real illusion of fame and then lost all sense of proportion. Then, in a matter of a few short months, he'd been written off as a failure. The new sense of meaning all this lent to his lyrics, combined with the sonic inspirations he'd absorbed in Long Island, made for an enormous change.

Now back in Brentwood, it was crunch time for Kara's Flowers. After the pressures of nearly falling apart, the foursome had decided to hold a meeting to determine whether they still had anything in common. Above all, one of the persistent difficulties was a disagreement over how they should sound.

"We had a lot of personal issues between the four of us to work out," Mickey would later admit to *Star Polish*. "Taste issues, creative issues . . . there was definitely tension because we were pulling in different ways. There were a lot of disparate tastes and feelings and, essentially, we had to decide to tough it out together, or else we'd fall apart."

Yet those new demos changed everything – and it was Mickey, most of all, who was intrigued by them. After all, Adam and Jesse's preferred sound now more closely matched his own. His longstanding passion for soul and Motown meant he'd looked up to the likes of Stevie Wonder for years, while the others were dubious. Now, however, it seemed as though the former rock loyalists had changed their tune.

"[The others] were definitely more narrow-minded when we were younger," Mickey elaborated. "That's just what happens. The more you're exposed to different kinds of music and the more you listen, the more you realise that anything can be appreciated . . . The breakthrough came from embracing hip-hop and R&B, Stevie Wonder and Herbie Hancock and the Police and Prince – things like that were hugely important influences for us. And when we started working in that sphere and aspiring to see what we could learn from those artists, I think that we became just happier. It was something that we were all passionate about."

He added, "As we've gotten older, we've been getting more and more open-minded – and now I don't think there's a single genre of music that any of us would dismiss as an influence."

The band had finally found their common ground. Now it seemed fitting to return to the studio and commit their new creative synergy to tape. They approached Ken Allardyce, explained that they'd made a change of direction and invited him to join them in the studio again to compile material for the attention of record labels. He obliged and consequently they found themselves at LA's Stagg Street Studios – previously used by a range of artists including Alanis Morissette, Red Hot Chili Peppers, Queens Of The Stone Age, Chaka Khan, Lou Reed, Pixies, Jill Sobule – original writer of later Katy Perry hit 'I Kissed A Girl' – and even Jessica Simpson.

Over the course of five days they produced 10 tracks, including reworked versions of 'If You Only Knew' and 'The Kid With Velvet Eyes' featuring different lyrics. The former channelled pure frustration, using road blocks and transport failures as metaphors for a lack of progress. While the track retained its emphasis on the disappointments doled out by the music industry, there was now an element of hope thanks to the presence of Adam's new girlfriend and emotional crutch, Jane Herman. According to him, thoughts of her are "tattooed" to his mind and obsessively thinking of his lover – one of the few things that stays right in his world full of wrongs – keeps him going through the most challenging of days.

'Good At Being Gone' sported an almost country twist and was another ode to Jane. Looking back to his fruitless Kara's Flowers tours and his stint in Dix Hills, he laments that all he's good at is being gone. Yet Jane provides stability and a perpetually strong influence in his life – while the whole world changes, she remains the same. While he can "roam" almost endlessly, he can rely on his leveller to be in the same place that he left her, reminding him of the pleasure of coming home.

'The Great Getaway' was another track about emotional escapism, depicting Adam and his lover flying through the sky on clouds that, in their eyes, had taken on the shape of a Chevrolet. As houses and cars slowly become smaller and smaller, before fading out of sight, they begin to "kiss the world goodbye" and venture to another place.

'Not Falling Apart' was in a similar surrealistic vein, with Adam retreating to a world underneath the waves. It was one of his final metaphors relating to water – indeed, within months of the recording, Mickey would insist, "I think we've let the maritime theme go . . . Adam's lyrical fascination with boats, oceans, storms et cetera has waned!"

At the same time, Ryan countered that climatic disturbances made a good metaphor for his personal relationships – as 'The Fog' demonstrated.

Adam sang of a couple yelling, screaming and driving each other crazy against the backdrop of a thick fog.

Also lurking in the background were more references to the music industry, as Adam spoke of career opportunities that had been sold along with someone's body and soul. The song additionally referenced abuse of prescription drugs as a reaction to tough times, a theme which would reappear on 'Simple Kind Of Lovely'. In the latter, Adam would make a controversial reference to "shooting the breeze" – street slang for taking heroin. It wasn't random creative licence either, because – as it would later emerge – Mickey had begun to descend into heroin addiction himself.

Loneliness was another common theme, depicted by a woman who blows kisses to no one in 'Everyday Goodbyes' and, in 'As Things Collide', a man whose elusive lover returns his hellos with goodbyes. Finally, in stark contrast to the new sounds showcased on the rest of the album, the group concluded by covering an old favourite – the Beatles' 'A Day In the Life'.

They were delighted with the new demos, but Allardyce approached their efforts with a more critical eye. "I felt that, as good as the songs were, there was a lack of direction in the group and a diversity of styles that didn't quite add up to defining a sound," he told the author. "In spite of that, we had a fun few days in the studio. In the two years since I'd worked with them, they and their songs had matured and although what we achieved was by no means a finished article, there was no mistaking their progress – I could even understand the lyrics!"

Admittedly, Adam's trademark delivery of nonsensical lyrics had raised a few eyebrows and wry smiles back in the early days, but although his way with words had since improved, he was still struggling to nail a definitive sound. The band had seen their hotchpotch of world culture and diverse musical influences as cosmopolitan and had been disheartened to find that, in contrast, Ken regarded it as a weak sense of identity.

But still, it was a starting point for the future. After a private showcase, *Meanstreet* magazine reported: "Fans can expect a boundary-crossing hybrid of anything from classic rock to Latin jazz, or country ballads to experimental emotional pop. Refusing to surrender to a rosy, power-pop genre mould, Kara's Flowers continues to surprise."

Neither were they afraid to break free from their defined roles. As they tirelessly promoted their songs on the California club scene – often agreeing to play for free – they would switch instruments as readily as they did genres.

As one fan, who caught them at the 800-capacity Glasshouse in the LA suburb of Pomona, told the author, "They opened with a Stevie Wonder song, but halfway through the show they performed Jimi Hendrix's 'Hey Joe', and everyone switched instruments. Adam was on drums, Ryan sang and took over Adam's guitar and Ryan's brother Josh got up onstage to play Jesse's guitar."

By the time they played the Rolling Stones song 'Beast Of Burden', everyone was joining in on vocal duties. "They were singing in crazy high voices," she continued, "and at one point Jesse and Adam shared a mic as they sang together, 'Pretty, pretty, pretty, pretty, pretty girls, c'mon, baby!' Unforgettable."

Although they were gradually establishing notoriety with gig-goers, the future for Kara's Flowers was far from certain. With enormous reluctance, Adam decided it was time for a back-up plan. He knew with "absolute certainty" that he wasn't cut out for academic life, which ruled out university. Creative at heart, however, he felt equally ill-suited to the menial minimum-wage jobs that were considered obvious choices for non-graduates.

Yet Kara's Flowers remained a small-fry underground group – just one of many with limited appeal. It had already failed once and it wasn't supporting him financially. If he wanted to follow his passion, he needed a regular income to spend on studio slots, as the recording sessions were far from over. Without qualifications, his choices were limited. He eventually landed a job as a waiter at the retro-style Johnny Rockets burger bar, but was fired within a matter of days – before he'd even completed his first shift, in fact.

"I trained and then I got the job and then I kept getting my shifts filled," he told *Contact Music*, "so I didn't actually work there, really. The manager took me in the back and said, 'Hey man, you haven't worked a day yet – you're fired.' I worked about three hours, screwed up about eight orders, got yelled at – I'm the worst waiter in the history of the world."

According to friends, Adam was a "narcissistic diva" – albeit a much-loved one – from the start and suffered from "the typical lead singer syndrome". Although he wasn't yet famous, his head was filled with gran-diose plans and the idea of deferring to a boss in a fast-food bar would wound his ego.

"He was a daydreamer," one old friend stated, "always thinking about where he'd rather be. He was extremely disorganised and couldn't be relied on to turn up on time – or even turn up at all. After all, why be one of the pack when you can be a leader and why blend into the background as a waiter when you can be a star?"

It was safe to say that Adam's future didn't lie in the service industry. As his mind kept skipping several steps ahead, he was already envisaging better things. Then family friend Barbara Hall – a TV writer and producer who co-owned her own production company – stepped in to bring him back down to earth. She offered him a position alongside her as writer's assistant for the nationally televised CBS drama *Judging Amy*. The show's central character was a single mother working as a juvenile court judge in Connecticut, struggling to navigate the heartbreaking decisions she must make in the name of justice.

Adam quickly capitalised on the family connection, cornering Barbara with a copy of his demo and persuading her to play a series of Kara's Flowers tracks on the show. On the first episode, 'Good At Being Gone', was the soundtrack to a child's abandonment by a hopelessly drug-addicted mother. Adam's heart may not have been in a desk job, but he was attentive enough to notice that the subject matter tied in perfectly with the song.

The following week, the drama continued as Amy intervened to prevent a doctor withholding medication from a severely ill infant – the soundtrack including 'The Great Getaway' and 'If You Only Knew'. It was extremely rare for songs that hadn't been officially released yet to debut to millions of viewers on a high-profile TV show – and the thrill of success spurred Adam on to write even more.

Around this time, Adam and Jane split up. By his own admission, his primary focus became writing tortured loss-of-love lyrics to detail his torment. As he half-heartedly researched juvenile court cases to build authenticity for Barbara's drama, he was also secretly scribbling down his own inner thoughts.

'These Days', for example, used war as a metaphor for a destructive rela-tionship. Questioning hatred in a lover's heart and violence in her eyes, he accuses her of waging war on everything he loved before pleading that he wanted the old days back. Dangerously, it isn't long before he gets them – with highly provocative emotional consequences. On 'July', Adam is lost in the "rip tides" of love, and the none-too-subtly titled 'Locked Up (Pleasure Fucker)' describes his entanglement with ill-advised post-break-up sex.

The latter displays how he feels tied to his former lover by an invisible thread, or trapped in an open prison – he's free to leave but his addiction binds him to her. He describes their sex sessions as offering him a vacation from himself – and yet this therapeutic escapism and total immersion in another person leaves him vulnerable to dependency. Although the couple is no longer together and, by definition, what they share is no-strings sex, the attachment is becoming ever stronger, leaving one or both liable to get hurt. He regards her as a dominant woman, claiming that she swoops in like a cougar. Although his significant other is still a teenager, she seems endowed with all the experience and confidence that greater maturity might bring. When it comes to oral sex he's unfaltering, singing that she's "hotter than a motherfucker" – and yet all the same traits that first attracted him to her now seem to be leading to his downfall. While reuniting confirms that there's certainly no passion lost between them, all of the differences that caused the relationship to disintegrate in the first place still prevail. While Adam becomes increasingly attached to her and begins to want her back fulltime, their former problems are now the proverbial elephant in the room, never too far away. That he'll get hurt is no longer a fear but a certainty. The only consolation is that he's been able to pour out his pain in the form of a song – as was true of the moment he found the willpower to break away from the destructive make-up/break-up cycle and leave Jane behind.

The poignant 'My Heart Won't Be Your Ragdoll Any More' talks of how he resists the temptation to give in to her demands to flit in and out of his life for uninvolved sex. In spite of weeks of previously hoping that he can talk her round and win her back, he has finally risen "off his knees" and is no longer powerless. Insisting that a "hot minute" isn't worth a "life of sorrow", he declares jubilantly that he no longer wants her back. He speaks of shutting his windows and locking his doors, a metaphor for insulating his heart from further hurt. Now an impenetrable fortress, with strength he hadn't known he possessed, he makes his message adamantly and unambiguously clear: he'll no longer fall prey to manipulative mind games. The grip his former love had over him has been broken, because he is no longer in love.

Meanwhile, 'Keep Your Head' was a reminder to himself not to masochistically let his heart reign over his head next time. Yet perhaps the experience, as painful as it had been, was a blessing in disguise. He'd never had his heart broken before, but now that he had, it formed the inspiration for his most emotional songwriting yet.

In the past, Kara's Flowers might have been regarded as obscenely over-privileged rich kids with nothing of real substance to sing about – but the tracks about Jane had provided a transformation. Their authenticity won over audiences who related to Adam's pain. He was no longer a mere performer – he now doubled as a therapist. Listeners could live out the emotions of their own past relationships vicariously losing themselves in the forceful matching emotions of each song. After all, there was nothing like raw tragedy to unite people. By daring to give away a small part of himself, by throwing his heart into the songs, he'd become universally relatable and understood.

Adam had been alternately both devastated and furious with Jane for what he saw as destroying their love. Yet now that he'd got creative mileage out of his emotions, he was beginning to understand why Jesse continually quoted Rage Against The Machine frontman Zach de la Rocha's catchphrase: "Anger is a gift."

Jesse would also quote the words of British politician, author and social activist Arthur Ponsonby, who had claimed that, "The absence of anger creates indifference – the most disastrous of human failings."

"I think that's a great point," Jesse had acknowledged, "and I think that indifference is just one of the many excuses a lot of people use to avoid facing sadness in the world. So get indignant and do something productive about the thing that makes you mad!"

It was good advice – at least in Adam's book. The most emotional relationship-inspired tracks were given a prominent position on their live playlist.

Slowly, the Kara's Flowers fanbase began to expand, with adults attending the shows as often as teenagers and the group unleashing new works in progress on the audience. In September 1999, 'However Whatever' was unveiled – a track lashing out at someone Adam perceived to be fake. The mystery person, whose falseness is described by the metaphor "plastic in their eyes", could have been a dig at Jane or, equally, at those the band felt had mismanaged them in their career. Through bitter experience, they'd grown to regard their industry as shallow and superficial – and by this point trusted no one. However, with eerie synchronicity, a friend was about to come into their lives who, thanks to a longstanding friendship, they trusted implicitly to manage their career.

The auspicious chain of events began with a show Kara's Flowers performed in support of Aquabats on New Year's Eve 1999. This momentous 'last show of the century', during which they performed a cover of Queen's 'We Are The Champions', attracted the attention of industry insider Tim Sommer.

An A&R rep and former TV host of the eighties, Sommer was little known as a producer and had no world-famous credits to his name. A deal with him was hardly synonymous with success, though he undoubtedly had contacts in the industry. He offered the band the chance of a demo deal – which was yet another source of uncertainty. With a back catalogue that included the likes of Elton John and Cher, MCA Records was not the most fashionable label for a band their age to sign to. With all that said, this was an opportunity Kara's Flowers was not about to turn down.

Consequently, the group headed out to New York to record a three-track taster of their sound. The CD included the newly written 'Sunday Morning', chronicling once again the obsessive, all-consuming emotions that Adam had felt towards Jane. By mid-2000, however, MCA had decided – despite Tim Sommer's urges to the contrary – to decline to sign the band.

The silver lining was that Jordan Feldstein, then a junior agent at ICM, had dropped in on one of the rehearsals – and was instantly intrigued. Jordan was the son of one of Adam's father's closest childhood friends and the brother of Adam's own friend, Jonah Hill – a boy with whom he'd shared his ambitions and fantasies of fame long before he'd had the courage to tell anyone else. Jonah and Jordan felt like family to him.

Within a month, Jordan had given up his job and agreed to manage the group fulltime. He had enormous faith in them – so much so that he was willing to sacrifice a regular wage based on nothing more than a possibility of getting them signed. It was exactly the kind of dedication they were seeking.

After they'd recorded a compilation CD of their best demos, Jordan shopped it to various labels – to a deafening silence. Other than the occasional polite rejection, most didn't even write back. Every major label they tried was uninterested, but Jordan persevered – this wasn't just business to him, but almost a question of family loyalty.

Yet just when even the doggedly tenacious Jordan looked set to give up, one morning in February 2001 the demo landed on the desk of Ben Berkman, Executive Vice President of newly founded label Octone. The CD was hardly professional – it wasn't even properly labelled – but the description of the songs caught his eye.

"It said something to the effect of, 'These dudes can be up all night playing cards with Stevie Wonder and partying with Sting!'" Ben recalled. "The description was exactly what it sounded like and it was exactly what I was looking for. Once I heard 'Sunday Morning', I just flipped."

Turning to the back of the CD sleeve, he did a double-take. Incredulously, he realised the tracks came from Kara's Flowers, whose original demos he'd heard during a stint working at Warner Bros. "I listened to it," he recalled begrudgingly, "thought it was garbage and threw it out of the sun roof of my car!"

He was astonished to find that the same group he'd once belittled was now making him speechless with excitement. As Octone was in its infant stages – he'd left his former company to branch out on his own – he was yet to sign a single act to the new label. Could Kara's Flowers be its inaugural stars?

To find out, he gathered up his colleague and jetted to LA to watch a live showcase at the Viper Room – a world famous hotspot for new talent to be discovered. "I was just blown away," he remarked. "They were only a four-piece; the singer played the guitar and seemed to be a very shy, shoe-gazing type, [but] I really believed that the band could be many people's favourite band if the right things fell into place . . . although they were very raw and lacking in terms of repertoire, we knew that they had the ability to galvanise fans out on the road and were capable of building communities around them in small pockets of the country."

To Berkman, they also stood out as unique. "It's rare to find a band as young as they were – at the time around 21 years old – who play drums and guitars but aren't a stereotypical rock band," he explained. "They're a rock band when you see them live, but not in the bashing away and screaming sense. My thought was that their kind of music was a bit advanced for its time, but that when the album came out, it would be exactly where music was going . . . I figured that there were so few of these bands that if we were to expose it, we could attract a lot of attention."

Many labels were fearful of taking a risk on artists that didn't fit the current mould. However Ben was not looking for what was in fashion – rather, he was looking for trendsetters who would set the *future* fashion.

While the large mainstream corporations were dubious, Octone had the creative control to choose its own acts without consulting a parent company. "We have our own money here, raised from private equity," he acknowledged, "so we make our own decisions as to the kind of artists that we want to sign."

Ben was keen to offer Kara's Flowers a contract on the spot – yet, as a newly founded and comparatively modest independent label, did Octone lack the marketing power of the big hitters? Could the band realistically achieve the fame they craved via this route?

As evidenced by their track record in other companies, Octone's founders were talented veterans with scores of connections in the industry. Plus, in spite of Octone's limited financial power, it had a co-venture deal with the much larger J Records subsidiary of the RCA Music Group. This meant that Octone took all the risk on producing a CD but, once an album started to sell profitably, it was eligible to be lifted into the joint venture where, as Berkman noted, it could benefit from the "vast resources [of J Records] to help promote the project".

This arrangement seemed to offer the best of both worlds – the band instinctively felt that under Octone's wing they would be a name rather than a number, that they would be regarded as artists instead of mere products on a conveyor belt. Independent labels were renowned for a liberal approach that gave artists more control over the work they presented to the world. Yet if they did succeed on their own terms, then a world of external financial resources would open up to them as well.

It was decided. Finally, seven years after Kara's Flowers were founded, they signed a deal that, unlike their ill-fated few months with Reprise, would be enduring. The burning question on many interviewers' lips was what had taken them so long?

In fact, aside from the disheartening early experiences and the group's slow evolution towards their own style, there had been another major factor stalling their progress. By his own admission, Mickey had been addicted to heroin. "You know how it is when you get addicted to a hard drug," he told *Star Polish*. "Basically my priority was heroin for a while and the band sort of came second . . . I just chose that one thing."

From the cynic's perspective, living in LA meant it had only been a matter of time. The club scene was notoriously rife with drugs and the young, impressionable foursome had been exposed to that world even earlier than their peers, playing over-21 concerts before they'd reached that age themselves. Yet now the group had started afresh with a label that had promised to promote them to the end, Mickey had broken the habit.

One of Adam's major complaints about Reprise had been that it hadn't taken the time to invest in sufficient live shows or build up a bigger fanbase before releasing the album. Octone prided itself on a very different approach.

"Many artists and albums aren't maximised because their record companies give up on them," Ben Berkman insisted. "They don't have the time or the patience to stick with it. We believe that if you have the right artist with a great live show, and you spend your money wisely by keeping them on the road and keep pushing, eventually the record will break."

Ben also placed an emphasis on the right repertoire – something all four felt they hadn't benefited from the first time round. "We want to distance ourselves from our album on Reprise," Ryan had claimed, "because we feel that our style is very different now than it was then."

To distance themselves from mistakes made in the past, they also decided to change their name. It was in part due to the insistence of their new label – but they hadn't needed much encouragement. "That name was a serious albatross," Mickey confessed later to *Associated Press*, "and we always hated it, almost since we had it – but we couldn't come up with a name we all agreed on."

As flattered as the much-admired Kara might have been to learn she was the source of inspiration, the reality was that her name often got lost in translation. "It was very difficult whenever people asked us the name of our band, for us to say clearly 'Kara's Flowers' and have them understand what we were saying," Ryan elaborated. "People would say 'Cars And Flowers', 'Carlos Flowers', 'Carson's Flowers' . . .'"

Those who did misunderstand the name had a tendency to mock it. In one subsequent web-chat, in which the boys took questions from fans, Adam had found himself ferociously defending their choices.

"Why did you trade one awful band name for another?" came the inflammatory taunt.

"Why did you take the time out of your life to ask that question?" Adam fired back. "What's in a name? The band makes the name, the name never makes the band. As we all know, the Beatles is a hideous name for a band – and they're the best band that ever lived."

Yet all four were relieved to leave the Kara's Flowers days behind. They debated fiercely over a replacement, considering the Funk Kings and Groovemeister, but ultimately rejected them as "we didn't want to spell out our style with a name". Instead, in a bid for something more mysterious and abstract, something that would draw an audience in without them knowing exactly why, they eventually agreed upon Maroon. There was more to the story – but, as the band would later tease, Billie Joe Armstrong was the only outsider who knew the full details and they remained a "closely guarded secret". No one else would ever find out!

They'd considered adding a '4' at the end to represent the number of band members – until discussion began about adding a fifth. Jesse had by now put down his guitar permanently in favour of keyboards, leaving Adam to take sole responsibility for the band's guitar sound. However Ben Berkman, who sensed a latent flamboyance in Adam, wanted him to be relieved of playing an instrument, "to free [him] up so that he could be the star I perceived him to be".

In Ben's eyes, hiding behind a guitar was inhibiting him and obscuring his frontman personality. Known as a diva in private, but still shy on occasion when it came to performing onstage, Ben aspired to coax the strong side of Adam out into the open. Enter James Valentine, a man who lived and breathed the guitar – someone who claimed he could never have survived adolescence without it.

One of five children, James – born on October 5, 1978 – had been raised in a devout Mormon family in the small town of Lincoln, Nebraska.

His mother, a former beauty queen and later a teacher, had eventually given up work to become a full-time housewife while his father taught Latin American literature at university. At home, both took their religious commitments seriously.

Growing up in the Mormon faith meant discipline and denial. Not only were alcohol and drugs strictly prohibited, so were coffee and tea. Pre-marital sex was forbidden, as well as any type of sex that did not lead to reproduction; as such, contraception was frowned upon.

The career path of a typical Mormon often involved undertaking a few years work as a missionary, spreading the word of God and enrolling new-comers into the faith before beginning their own working life. For some, it was considered an obligation – almost a spiritual debt that, in the name of good karma, had to be repaid.

Both of James' parents would go on to teach at the Brigham Young University in Utah – owned by the Church of Jesus Christ of Latter Day Saints, founders of the Mormon faith – and would consequently adminis-ter missionary duties in the students' curriculum. On average, 78 per cent of all men attending would interrupt their studies for two years to comply with these duties.

Yet the church's fundamentalists had a reputation of which many dis-approved. It was controversial that polygamy was tolerated by religious law – in fact, the university's founder, Brigham Young himself, had married a total of 55 wives. Many viewed this as a selective interpretation of morality, leaving the Mormon faith deeply flawed.

Even at James' young age, the monumental list of rules was overwhelm-ing; being a good Mormon seemed to mean sacrificing everything that was enjoyable in life. Yet he quickly developed a distraction from the religious indoctrination at home: music.

His elder brother, Christopher, six years his senior, was involved in a high school band, with he and his friends often using the family's basement as a rehearsal room. "As a little kid, I used to sit at the top of the basement stairs and listen to them rehearse for hours," James later recalled. "I would wait for them to leave and make noise on all their instruments!"

The instrument he felt most drawn to was the drum kit – but he had some competition in the shape of his best friend across the street. "His mom bought him a drum kit before my parents would," James explained, "so he became a drummer in the band. We had started to conceptualise. That was OK though. My brother had been playing me a lot of tapes – specifically *Moving Pictures* by Rush – and that had gotten me excited about playing the guitar."

After a few weeks of pester power, his parents eventually gave in, buying 13-year-old James his own guitar and enrolling him on an eight-week crash course at the music store in his local mall. The lessons sparked an obsession, with his mother recalling admiringly later: "We never had to tell him to practise. In fact, we were more likely to tell him to put it down!"

"[Being a guitar hero] was my obsession," he would later admit to *Ultimate Guitar*. "When I was a kid, I did not care about the song. I was waiting for the solo, of course! It was about the riff and I still can't remember lyrics because I'm usually listening to that other part of the song."

As James grew older, he was perceived to be honest, calm, democratic and moral, and to possess leadership qualities – assets which saw him appointed President of Lincoln Southeast High's student council. Yet music remained his passion and he began to seriously consider becoming a jazz musician.

"When I was in high school, I guess the Holy Trinity for me was Pat Metheny, Bill Frisell and John Scofield," he recalled. "Those were really my guys. Early on, I really saw myself pursuing instrumental music . . . that was mostly what I listened to . . . I was kind of known as the jazz guy."

To channel his obsession still further, he joined the school's jazz band where, in his enthusiasm, he drowned out most of the other students. His tutor, Mr Olmsted, would continually ask him to turn the sound down.

However, in spite of his jazz focus, James was much in demand with the local rock groups. Surprisingly for such a quiet, religious and traditionally conservative state, Nebraska had given birth to a thriving music scene, with electropop groups such as the Faint choosing to remain in residence even post-fame. One of the bands that hoped to emulate that level of fame, Montay, specialised in covers of grunge hits, mixed in with the occasional original tune. James would briefly find himself their lead guitarist, before an equally brief stint in the rock group Mondello.

Yet when it came to graduation from high school, James found himself at an inevitable crossroads. He couldn't foresee himself giving up guitar, but the obvious national choice for an aspiring musician like himself – the Berklee College of Music in Boston – was decidedly out of his price range. His enthusiasm was also tempered by warnings he'd received that "making a living as a musician was impossible", with the exception of a select few. He feared that paying the bills by playing the instrument he adored was an unrealistic dream.

James compromised by enrolling on a more affordable nine-week summer school at Berklee in 1996. The college was the largest independent music school in the world, with past alumni boasting a combined total of 229 Grammy Awards. At their intensive guitar camp, with world-class instructors, he would first meet the soon-to-be-famous John Mayer. Back in those early days, John still lived with his parents and was scraping a living as a petrol-station attendant. But to James, he instantly stood out as a promising blues guitarist – and, of course, a competitor. "He won the big scholarship prize," James would later tell *Ultimate Guitar*, "the son of a bitch!"

On returning home, James was even more conflicted than before. Believing music was far from a secure career path, he reluctantly enrolled at the University of Nebraska on a much more affordable degree in PR and advertising, resolving to demote music to the status of a hobby. Yet he couldn't give it up entirely.

"I liked my classes," he recalled, "but every spare moment was devoted to music . . . I don't know if I would have survived adolescence without the guitar."

His star rose in the Midwest when he began touring the region with his new group, Kid Quarkstar. After months of playing college parties and bars with them – the perks of the latter being free underage entry to over-21 concerts – James dropped out of university to focus fulltime on the group. It was against all the advice of his anxious parents, who wanted him to follow the conventional path.

Yet they came around – and he offered guitar tuition around the neighbourhood to make ends meet. For a nail-biting moment, it soon looked as though his family might have been right when Kid Quarkstar fizzled out – but then another group, Square, "rose from the ashes" to take its place.

The band comprised vocalist and keyboardist Sean Beste, drummer Ryland Steen and James on guitar – three friends who stood out for their unusual fusion of jazz and rock. Meanwhile Sean's distinctively high voice added another unexpected dimension, inviting comparisons to Jay Kay of Jamiroquai. The advantage they held was that they sounded like no one else on the Lincoln music scene, and they quickly built up a fanbase.

Their material was also an attraction. Songs included 'Political Cop', accusing corrupt policemen of turning law enforcement into oppression, and '26', about the agonising uncertainty of not knowing whether one's life goals will ever become a reality. Their unique brand of musicianship attracted the attention of several record companies, but the trio were hesitant, believing they should make a full-length album first without the impediment of interfering label bosses.

While they did so, Sean secretly entered them into a nationwide Battle of the Bands contest founded by strings manufacturer Ernie Ball. "Sean was embarrassed even to tell us that he entered us," James recalled for *OC Weekly*. "Really, we were more embarrassed about it than anything else – winning was the last thing on our minds."

Pitted against almost 6,000 other acts, the odds were certainly high. Yet the incredulous trio found themselves sailing through preliminary round after round until their group was one of just four finalists left.

"Having a contest based around music is pretty weird anyway," James mused as he waited for the judges – a team including Lit, Save Ferris, Reel Big Fish and CC DeVille of Poison – to announce the winner. "It's like I was back competing in [school] sports."

Reel Big Fish, along with several others, awarded Square a perfect 10 out of 10. To James' astonishment, it was announced that they were the triumphant band and had won $25,000 worth of prize money.

Yet within minutes, a shadow was cast over his elation. Feeling a tap on his shoulder, he turned round to see one of his biggest idols standing behind him – but he wasn't exactly there to offer his congratulations.

"Dweezil Zappa, who was MC'ing the whole thing, pulled us aside and said, 'It's all downhill from here, guys,'" James recalled. "He basically told us, 'Good luck, but go home' – and that was our first exposure to *that* scene – all these jaded musicians who'd been hurt by their livelihood."

Fortunately for James, he didn't listen. In fact, there was no argument among the trio about how they should invest their winnings. Within days, James, Sean and Ryland had grabbed a few possessions, loaded them into a battered van and driven at breakneck speed down the highway to freedom.

Freedom meant California, of course. The Battle of the Bands contest had taken place in LA, the heart of the West Coast music scene, and although they couldn't afford to be that close to the city they were able to settle in Anaheim, a 40-mile commute away. Aside from the occasional frivolous purchase, such as annual season tickets to Disneyland, all of their prize money was spent on the move. They were serious about making it in the business.

At first all three were overwhelmed by the sheer scale of the industry for those on the verge of fame. "If we played this much back in Lincoln," Sean would retort after a long string of concerts, "we'd be the house band in every single club, [but] at least there's an actual music scene here."

Square slowly began to enjoy the first flushes of fame, recording a demo CD with a local producer and performing showcases to record companies. However, once the novelty of their Battle of the Bands win faded from public consciousness, it was nothing more than a credit on their CV. Their fusion tones – precisely what had attracted listeners to them back in Nebraska – were unnerving some moguls who, according to James, perceived them as having a "weird" sound. As the months passed, it became evident that they were seen as too weird to even sign – and James had to get inventive about ways to become more musically accessible. Then a gig he'd attended by chance answered his prayers.

Although his band had stopped trying their luck on the club scene, there was one competitor that stood out to him as fascinating: Kara's Flowers. James' loyalty lay with Square, but when Aaron of Reel Big Fish had taken him to their show at the Glasshouse, he instantly – and a little guiltily – visualised himself in the group. Just as a man in a relationship might discreetly indulge in mental masturbation at the sight of an attractive woman behind his girlfriend's back – or, as the early Kara's Flowers lyrically described it, a "mental mind fuck" – James was fantasising about cheating on his band by taking his musicianship somewhere else.

"I knew straight away when I saw them," he later recalled, "that I could be the guitar player this band needed." Moreover, there was no doubt in his mind that they needed one. "I understood before I even knew the guys how I was gonna fit in," he continued. "The first time I saw them play, it was clear at certain times that Adam was pulling the guitar behind him, Bruce Springsteen style, and then playing keyboards and then rushing back to throw it on within the same song. He'd play the guitar on the chorus and he was playing piano on the verses – so from the very first time I saw exactly how I was gonna fit in."

Back then, it had just been a fantasy – but James was adamant that he belonged with them, not least because he felt they were head and shoulders above any of their peers. In his eyes, they were of the calibre he'd once mistakenly imagined every LA artist to be.

"I had the idea in my head that all the bands playing out in LA were going to be amazing," he later told *Fender* of his idealistic early notions, "the best musicians in the world! I couldn't have been more wrong – until I saw Kara's Flowers . . . they were hands down the best band I had seen since I moved to LA. I could sense that they weren't complete [and] I somehow knew I was going to be in the band, even though I was still completely devoted to Square."

He'd hidden this streak of emotional infidelity from his bandmates, but somehow they'd been having premonitions about his future too. "If Square didn't happen in a timely fashion," Sean had glumly forecast, "I knew that James or Ryland would get snatched up by other bands."

It hadn't helped that the honeymoon period for the group was undoubtedly over. James and Sean had been increasingly argumentative, their tensions inflamed still further by their financial meltdown. While they'd gained a reputation in the regional media as the 'OC buzz band' – an affectionate nickname that referred to their base in Orange County – the hype hadn't translated to a record deal and their prize money was slowly, but surely, dwindling away.

Now every dollar they earned was being poured back into their dream, with the purchase of equipment and studio time bearing ever-heftier price tags. Unlike the boys from Kara's Flowers, James had lacked the financial backing of wealthy parents – and modest handouts from his own family had been exhausted long ago. Meanwhile, the cost of living was far higher than anything Square had encountered in Nebraska and they were coming dangerously close to returning home in defeat.

James was so tenacious that, given the choice between an evening meal and a packet of strings, he'd almost certainly have chosen the latter. Yet these were fast becoming real-life decisions – and the irony was that the so-called buzz band, whose name was on everyone's lips, were impoverished to the point that they could barely afford to eat.

One journalist, Rick Kane from *OC Weekly*, had taken James and Sean for an interview over lunch and had seen them tuck in ravenously to the restaurant's fare – for those who'd been surviving on baked beans for weeks, it was almost a palatial feast.

"They wolfed down curry platters like they hadn't seen food for days," Kane would recall incredulously, perhaps unaware of just how true to life that description was.

It was make or break time – if James wasn't saved by a miracle, he'd almost certainly have to follow Zappa's advice and dejectedly make his way home. "I was starting to mount a pretty impressive credit card debt," he'd later wince. "However at the same time I was surrounded by an amazing circle of musicians and was having the time of my life."

Desperate to maintain the lifestyle he loved, he found his mind flitting back to Kara's Flowers – if they could only open for the band, with their impressive Southern California following, Square might be able to attract the attention of a well-connected scenester to kick-start their career. At the very least, they could gain some new fans.

James also still harboured secret fantasies about impressing them with his technical expertise and being invited to join the band. Sooner than he'd imagined, that opportunity came.

"Through some fortuitous connections, I arranged for Square to open for Kara's Flowers," he recalled. "I felt it would be good for Square to play in front of their fans, but I also think I secretly wanted them to see me play – I know how evil and Machiavellian that sounds! I could tell as soon as we started playing that they were indeed impressed."

A cunning James lured the group back to the house he shared with Sean and Ryland later that night, using the latter's cousin and "her really cute friends" as bait. Just as he'd hoped, he and Kara's Flowers instantly bonded over shared influences, such as Trey Anastasio from the group Phish – someone both he and Adam would rave about late into the night.

Adam and James intrigued each other because of the different perspectives each brought to their music. James knew little about rock guitar, the background from which Kara's Flowers had originated, while his jazz, funk and fusion influences matched Adam's vision for the future of his own band. Each had different strengths, different areas of knowledge and expertise – and in the end they would complement one another.

That night was a scintillating exchange of creative ideas, holding the prospect of collaborations that might break musical boundaries. However, while those possibilities had been racing ahead in James' mind, their lofty heights wouldn't be reached yet.

His next chance to work with the group was under the distinctly unglamorous job description of guitar technician – but with his funds now almost non-existent, he felt obliged to take on the role. It was the summer of 2000 and Kara's Flowers, in the midst of recording the demos that would get them signed to Octone, were still unaccustomed to going into the studio totally alone. In fact, they barely knew how to change their own strings.

"They really did not know anything about maintenance of their own guitars," James would laugh incredulously to the *Miami New Times*. "I think it's just a result of having been signed to a record deal when they were like 16 years old. So when they were making their first record, they already had guys here changing their strings and taking care of their guitars. So when they went to go do that recording session and they weren't on a label any more and didn't really have those extra resources, they didn't really know what to do. I was around and they asked me to change the strings on their guitars! They basically didn't know how to. It was maintenance work and I was of course near poverty at the time . . . !"

Taking on the status of hired help, taking care of menial tasks while the others acted like stars, was an almost demeaning experience for James. Yet the silver lining of this arrangement would be the chance of future collaborations.

His persistence paid off. By 2001, when Ben Berkman had his brainwave about relieving Adam from the restrictions of the guitar, James had already grabbed the opportunity to ingratiate himself into Kara's Flowers' inner circle. He was the most obvious addition to the family.

When the moment he'd longed for finally came, James was on an emotional rollercoaster. The primary emotion was excitement, but the contradictory feelings of uncertainty, insecurity and guilt were gnawing away at him. His affair had been discovered, his infidelity exposed. Now he was set to leave behind his bandmates to whom he had promised his loyalty.

"It was tough for me to make that decision," he later recalled the agony. "I didn't want to abandon those guys – we moved out to LA together. But it seemed like it was somehow my destiny."

5

And Then There Were Five

WITH five members in the group, Maroon 5 was now truly born. Just as they prepared to enter the studio under their new moniker, however, their lives were disrupted by the events of one unforgettable day: September 11, 2001.

Out of tragedy was born hope and compassion, while the shared experience of loss created a community spirit which saw large numbers of New Yorkers pull together. War had reinforced the need for solidarity and, in honour of the tragedy, Adam and Jesse got matching dove tattoos, symbolising peace.

The events of 9/11 offered a poignant parallel with their own lives. Like the Twin Towers, Kara's Flowers and the ill-fated deal with Reprise had crashed and burned – but Maroon 5 had risen from the ashes, and their initial failure only made them all the more determined to succeed. In subsequent interviews, the group would tell anyone who would listen that they were grateful for their failures the first time round; it was with lighter hearts that they looked towards their first album as a five-piece.

Octone had initially sought after Nile Rodgers as a producer – whose credits included work with Diana Ross, David Bowie and Duran Duran – but they were forced to pull out when he commanded a figure more than three times their budget.

"We just couldn't afford it," Ben Berkman recalled. "We needed to keep it down to about $100–150,000." Instead, they turned their attentions to Matt Wallace, who was famed for his work with Faith No More, and Mark Endert, who'd produced for Madonna. The combination would provide an intriguing balance of pop and rock styles.

The backdrop to recording was an atmosphere of heightened emotions

– in Adam's case, both grief and elation. He was experiencing the final death throes of his on-off relationship with Jane, which had seemingly reached a point of no return several times only for the pair to reunite again. This time, however, they knew it was permanently over.

Both were getting on an aeroplane to take them in separate directions. He was headed for the studio while Jane was leaving town to pursue her fashion writing career. While Adam was deliriously excited about getting back into the studio, he felt pangs of regret that his first love had been written out of his life. Yet the old adage that says one door closes and another one opens was the bittersweet truth for Adam – at least on the day that 'This Love' came to fruition. The track exorcised his feelings about the final goodbye, but he would remain consumed by memories of Jane. He would later confess that "90 to 100 per cent" of his songwriting inspiration came from his love – and at times hate – of the fairer sex, and the Maroon 5 debut album was no exception.

The track-list followed the trajectory of an archetypal passionate love affair – a couple exchanging furious, heated words of aggression before apologising profusely and pleading forgiveness. Love turns to hate and back again with dizzying speed.

"It is definitely a concept record," Adam told *Pure Songwriters*, "making the statement, 'This relationship isn't working. It isn't working. I hate you. You're a bitch. Fuck you, but I love you and you're amazing and I hope things can work out but if they can't, then fuck you.' Then finally at the end it's like, 'All right, it's not gonna work out, but let's do this peacefully.'"

To capture an emotional ending, the group also revived 'Sweetest Goodbye', an older track that dated back to Adam and Jane's first break-up. Strongly influenced by the album *The Miseducation Of Lauryn Hill,* the studio version featured Adam on guitar.

The high moments of the relationship were captured in tracks such as 'Secret', but the drama soon resurfaced in 'Through With You' and 'Not Coming Home'. "We wanted a straight ahead, overdriven, aggressive sort of vibe that I think complements the darker lyrics of those songs," James revealed. "We wanted to be aggressive and slam hard."

'Through With You' sees Adam suffering his lover's ambivalence and at times her indifference – a woman who takes his hand just to give it back, who declares love while her actions suggest the very opposite. It's Adam's chance to vent his frustrations, make his feelings known and take his power back, achieved by the scornful delivery of the words "through with you".

'Not Coming Home' acts as the sequel to 'My Heart Won't Be Your Ragdoll Anymore'. Adam claims he would have done anything to end a lover's suffering, but she is cold, abusive and unresponsive, and would "rather walk away". Now he is doing the same – furiously asserting the upper hand with a declaration of emotional freedom. He cuts the ties of dependency and moves on – although not quite enough to avoid a little satisfaction from the revenge, while some rocky Red Hot Chili Peppers-style guitars set the mood.

So has he truly moved on, or does he feel the need to prove it purely to hurt his ex? In other moments, he falls back into infatuation: in 'Tangled Up', he apologises for his angry outbursts and accepts the lion's share of the blame; in 'Must Get Out', which intentionally channels Andy Summers' guitar sound in the Police, he is a slave to Jane's will and finds himself hanging on while she takes a break and in 'Shiver', he is fully immersed in the toxic affair, sexually infatuated in spite of his acknowledgment that the woman he loves is the "queen of run-around", someone who will casually chew him up and spit him out.

'The Sun' confirms the entire theme of the album, where he states that he hates to love Jane and loves to hate her – consequently they go back and forth, breaking up and getting back together like a broken CD player blaring out the same repetitive pattern of sounds. However, on the jazzy, piano-infused 'Sunday Morning' – the song that got Maroon 5 signed – all the anguish seems to be forgotten, until the next time.

When it came time to pen the Savage Garden sound-alike 'She Will Be Loved', Adam had backed away from the relationship once and for all and, as a reaction to the pain of the break-up, had entered a phase of total disassociation.

"I went through a period where I was kind of emotionally detached from everyone," he told *Pure Songwriters*, "especially girls – so I kind of started to focus on other people's relationships to find inspiration because I wasn't finding anyone in my own life. 'She Will Be Loved' was actually written from a friend's perspective." Although the identity of the friend was never publicly disclosed, the track is the only one on which James has a co-writing credit.

Regrettably for Adam, his love life had been too turbulent to pen many optimistic tracks. There was another barrier to his progress when his ADHD returned in full force. "He's very impulsive and he's not very patient," James would recall of his progress in the studio. "He's not gonna sit around and fiddle with the amp forever."

While James admiringly acknowledged that Adam was lightning fast when it came to creating new ideas – "He's got so many coming in that he's already singing background vocals in his head while we're still tracking guitars!" – the challenge for Adam lay in focusing in on one specific idea for long enough to develop it.

To have his head chaotically crowded with ideas that all seemed to pop into his consciousness at once, each stalling the progress of the others, was more of a hindrance than a help. It was a scenario akin to that of hopeless Homer Simpson, the cartoon figure who comically lamented, "Every time I learn something new, it pushes some old stuff out of my brain!"

"I remember very definitely being stuck and not being able to focus," Adam revealed to About.com. "I had 30 ideas floating through my mind and just couldn't document them. I went back to the doctor to discuss my symptoms and learned that I still had ADHD and that it could affect me as a young adult or adult. Once I knew that I still had it, I was able to work with my doctor to help manage my symptoms."

This would involve a prescription of concentration enhancing drugs – which, as it happened, arrived just in time.

In spite of seeing potential in all of the tracks, Octone's bosses were still dissatisfied. The first single was of momentous importance, as it would be the sound that introduced Maroon 5 to the world. Their agonisingly vague brief was for a stronger, more striking song that stood out as a hit. Adam was contractually obligated to deliver.

The resulting track questions how an unnamed person could dare to be so condescending and critical, vowing that if they deem his behaviour unacceptable then his reaction will be to get "very physical". However, the latter part of the song seems to refer to the ending of a personal relationship, where he asks if it burns to learn that he now has the upper hand of control and taunts the woman concerned that she may never find a lover as good as him.

The track had absolutely nothing to do with Adam's life – it was penned in the heat of an imminent deadline and was a purely fictional tale. However, it had powerful potential to be misunderstood – in the same breath as addressing a lover clutching her pillow and writhing in a "naked sweat", he was threatening to get physical and warning someone to watch their step. The most controversial aspect of the song was the widely-held perception that it was about domestic violence, yet Adam soon dispelled that myth, countering, "That song comes sheerly from wanting to throw something."

The references to violence were symbolic of the resentment he felt at being forced to be "creative on demand". He had felt suffocated by the pressure he was under to produce a masterpiece and the anger came flowing out – but he would be adamant in subsequent interviews that he did not condone physical violence. "It was the eleventh hour and the label wanted more songs – it was the last straw," he explained to MTV. "I was just pissed."

He would later elaborate: "It's about not wanting to write songs and being forced to write songs to the point of taking drugs in order to get those songs done. It takes a lot of Dexedrine, Ritalin, whatever you want to call it – I call it speed. I didn't want to write any more songs and the album demanded more of us. I'm glad they did, because . . . when we're actually able to focus, we're a force to be reckoned with."

It wouldn't be long before he would rebel again, taking issue with the label's choice of 'Harder To Breathe' for the debut single. Yet Adam – who by now had a cupboard full of prescription pills to boost his songwriting abilities – was still glad that the final sessions had come to a close and the pressure to perform was off.

As Ryan would later recall, their anxiousness to produce their best work, without any album fillers, had been nerve-racking. "We wanted to have an entire album full of songs that could be a hit," he explained. "No throwaways. At least in our minds, every song had to be slamming. Then we had to work really hard to make sure it sounds the best it can sound, with the resources we had. We weren't fucking around."

While the deadlines had now been removed and it felt as though a weight had been lifted from their backs, they didn't revel in the glory of what they'd created for long. It was time for stage two – "touring our butts off" – and that was where the hard work would really begin.

Before Octone released the album, Ben Berkman's priority was to build a ready-made fanbase – an army of devotees who would wait in hungry anticipation for its release. Taking a traditional grass-roots approach, he wanted to market Maroon 5 first as a live personality, building on their small group of about a thousand local loyalists until they were admired nation-wide. Achieving this, of course, meant visiting every major city in America.

"I think we spend more money on tour support than just about any label in the business," Ben told *Hit Quarters*. "Our tour support programs are very aggressive and competitive compared to those of the majors. When we find artists, we ask them if they are willing to get into a van and be on the road for a year or even a year and a half, because that's what it's going to take. And when they ask us if we are willing to pay for it and we say yes, that's often the deal maker right there. You have to be an excellent live band, because [that's] the way we seek to promote our artists."

It matched Adam's view exactly. In his eyes, any other route was reserved for novelty acts, bubblegum pop singers and charlatans. "Labels can launch pop singers really easily," he opined to *Pure Songwriters* scath-ingly. "It just involves a lot of money and throwing it at everybody and having a pretty face and a catchy song that you hire a songwriter to write. It's simple. That kind of formula's really easy, but as far as a rock'n'roll band, you've gotta go hit the road!"

For Adam, it was in sweaty nightclubs, with crowds packed almost air-tight into the room, where the magic happened. Moreover with down-loads – illegal or otherwise – now an undeniable part of pop culture, developing their live experience was a band's best investment when it came to securing survival. A buzz band whose single had been casually downloaded onto countless laptop track-lists meant nothing if the connec-tion between themselves and their fans was superficial, based on good looks or catchy tunes alone.

As Adam would knowingly concede later, it wasn't unhelpful that the foursome were all "quite good-looking", but the difference between a popular band and a successful one with an appropriate measure of longev-ity lay not in eye-candy, but in the bond they'd built with audiences.

"The obsession with celebrity has overshadowed substance," Adam would argue in *USA Today*. "There's a lot of music out there, but not a lot of people who can actually play live."

To him, many pop stars were disposable, their fame often lasting as long as their debut hit remained fashionable. With the brains of the best – and most expensive – producers behind them, certain beats were guaranteed to be a hit, irrespective of the face and body that modelled the sound. Just as a fashion model was a clothes horse, a vocalist was a walking CD rack sold via mirages of Photoshopped beauty. They sported hair extensions, fake nails and layers of make-up so thick that it obscured their natural features. Meanwhile, their voices were flatteringly disguised by a combination of computerised enhancements and Auto-Tune. Stripped down, they were doubtless unrecognisable – all that was left was a jaded salesperson, chewed up and spat out by the fame game – who may or may not be able to carry a tune. Their faces and bodies may well have been a work of art – but were they real or merely the product of stylists, or even surgeons? Where was the heart and soul?

It was Adam's view that such singers were the whores – or perhaps more politely, brand ambassadors – of multimillion dollar corporations, arguably manipulated by record label 'pimps' for obscene amounts of profit. When the main selling point of a singer was his or her looks, their shelf lives would be inevitably short. Stories in the mass media would not centre on their debatable talent, but on the status of a relationship or the hemline of a dress – more likely to adorn tabloid gossip columns than playlists. When the foundations of their careers were built on something as transitory as sex appeal, they ultimately had an expiry date and their futures were as fragile as a house of cards.

Adam, in contrast, wanted to find fame the hard way – building his reputation brick by brick. He knew he wasn't aesthetically challenged, but neither were many other new hopefuls. What would set him apart was his goal of communicating heart, soul and passion through the music, relying on instruments to do the job rather than processed beats. To him, any other way of spreading the message would render him replaceable.

Knowing that fame wouldn't fall into their laps, Maroon 5 tirelessly toured the country. Yet perhaps Adam should have been careful what he'd wished for because, while there was none of the superficiality of celebrity culture about his first few months on the road, the experience was devoid of glamour too.

Strapped for cash and confined to a cramped van that alternately smelt of "petrol and piss", they were hardly travelling in style. Not only were there no luxury leather seats, but there were no beds either, making overnight journeys unbearable.

"Van tours," James would declare, "are definitely not for the weak."

Ultimately, what made each arduous trip worthwhile – and worth sacrificing the familiar comforts of family and friends – was the buzz they'd built in all corners of the USA. This truly was the grass-roots approach.

"We'd been out on the road since February 2002, before we even had a release date," Ryan would tell MTV. "People were coming up to us saying, 'I want to buy your album, but I don't know where to get it.'"

The mystery was solved on June 25, 2002, when *Songs About Jane* first hit the shops. Its release came just as the group was preparing for the Jeep World Outside Festival tour, which would see them support artists such as Sheryl Crow.

Thanks to their extended fanbase built up from months of shows, they sold 1,000 copies in the first week – but still had a long way to go. The media response to the album was lukewarm at best.

"It's hard to imagine Maroon 5 getting too far with their current sound," *Pop Matters* asserted dismissively, before accusing them of a lack of originality. "Adam Levine sounds so much like Jason Kay on this album that one could be forgiven for thinking that Jamiroquai had slid down the pipes a little further."

Jamiroquai, the review insisted, had "diluted" Stevie Wonder – and it seemed as though Maroon 5 were taking the same road. After diminishing the album overall as a "funk-lite" blend of the likes of Britney Spears and the Backstreet Boys, it sneered, "Maroon 5 won't ever be mistaken for having laid down any real rock or soul on this album . . . those guys are light-weights when it gets down to it."

It didn't help that, for the debut single, Octone had chosen the pop-flavoured 'Harder To Breathe' – a decision about which Adam was decidedly ambivalent. "I didn't love or hate the song," he'd tell *USA Today*, "and I didn't care if it got on the album. We have a lot of pop songs on our record and the idea was to start out with something different. Why come out of the gate with another pop song by another pop band?"

Adding to his frustration, the album as a whole would widely be accused of failing to break new musical ground – exactly the perception they had sought to avoid. In the UK, reluctant praise from *The Guardian* could barely have been more muted, with notoriously caustic reviewer Caroline Sullivan begrudgingly stating that "the first album isn't as useless as one would hope". Meanwhile, the boys may well have cringed to read that, in her eyes, they were well-suited to "the Busted market".

With this type of press preceding it, the TV debut of 'Harder to Breathe' was already a source of embarrassment for Adam. He'd stayed awake until four in the morning to watch it on VH1, but found it an anticlimax. "That was kinda lacklustre," he'd complain. "I'm not crazy about the video. It's just boring."

Admittedly, Octone had spent just $55,000 on the simple performance video – by the standards of the music world, a frugal sum indeed – but Adam's candid dislike for it wasn't helping to drum up enthusiasm. One of the markets Octone had hoped to focus on was rock, but the track was virtually ignored by MTV2 listeners. As the months passed, sales remained disappointingly low and a mention of the band would generally be met with a blank stare and the question 'Maroon who?' – followed by a query as to whether it was a number on a paint chart.

In spite of the lacklustre reception, Ben Berkman was quietly confident, insisting he'd predicted all along that the track would be a slow burner. "I knew it was going to be a really slow build-up because it was a song that people wouldn't get sick of and could therefore be played many, many times because it didn't sound like anything else out there."

Maroon 5 themselves were not quite so confident. During this critical make-or-break moment, Octone was reduced to giving away copies of the album virtually for free.

"We sold live tickets really cheaply in the markets we had airplay in and we even sold the album for the price of the frequency of the radio station, like 91 cents for 91X," Ben recalled. "We also asked programme directors to announce that the album could be bought for 91 cents at a given independent retailer every time they aired the single."

What might initially have seemed like career suicide was in fact an effective PR campaign, guaranteeing everyone would know their name. At under a dollar, who could resist? Meanwhile, if the album resonated with listeners, there was all the more chance that they'd become a fan and support them on their second album – and at full price next time.

Octone's priority, unlike other labels the group had very vocally criticised in the past, was not about making a quick buck – they were in it for the long haul. Other industries regularly invested heavily and made financial sacrifices for years before seeing any results – why should music be any different? Every scarcely affordable promotion in the short term was an investment for the future.

By January 2003, Maroon 5's debut album had sold 50,000 copies. That was when the joint venture with J Records – activated as soon as a band's prospects began to look promising – kicked in. Its financial backing allowed Octone to cross over from rock to mainstream pop radio.

Once they stepped out of the shadows, the reaction was instant. MTV described the band as a cross between Justin Timberlake – someone the Maroon 5 boys had fiercely debated over a long van tour, before coming to the decision that he was "a legend" – and Red Hot Chili Peppers. Meanwhile, *Guitar One* admiringly declared them "rock's first neo-soul band". In spite of the naysayers, it seemed that there were some who *did* feel they were breaking musical boundaries.

By this time, they'd played over 250 shows under the Maroon 5 moniker and were slowly but surely gathering momentum. As *Spin* would predict: "You know when you find a band before anyone else does and a few months after, everybody is screaming their name? That band is Maroon 5."

Rather than becoming complacent at the first sign of success, the group spent much of 2003 touring relentlessly to try to change their unsung status. They toured with Matchbox 20 and Sugar Ray in April and performed a series of co-headlining shows with Jason Mraz in June. The following month they'd join Counting Crows and John Mayer for an amphitheatre tour of the US, secured partly by James' relationship with John.

"To be honest, he was the first real avid supporter of the band that was a big name," Adam confessed to *Live Daily*. "He genuinely loved the music and walked into our dressing room [just to say] 'I love your record.' I think he was the first person to really jump on board."

Adam, Ryan, Jesse and Mickey's gratitude towards James for introducing them to Mayer – and indeed for introducing John to their music – earned him some brownie points and made him feel like one of the pack at last. "James did feel a little awkward to begin with, simply because everyone else in that group had known each other for years," a friend told the author. "They were all welcoming to him, but he still felt like the newcomer. This John Mayer tour rebalanced the scales."

Then followed tours with soul singer Nikka Costa and, in September, Gavin DeGraw. Yet it wasn't until October that *Spin*'s ambitious predictions for the group came true. After a 16-month publicity campaign, 'Harder To Breathe' finally hit the mainstream chart's top 40, peaking at number 18. By October 27, the CD had been released in the UK too. The same month, *Songs About Jane* was re-released, but it wasn't until the second single, 'This Love', that the band's popularity exploded.

"It just galvanised everything," J Records exec Tom Carson stated. "It made the band stars . . . that was the launching pad to everything else." It was also remixed by Mark Endert, who glossed over its wide spectrum of influences with a pop sheen that would lend itself well to commercial radio.

Yet one thing that clearly distinguished it from its squeaky-clean pop peers was its overtly sexual lyrics. "Yep, that's sexual all right," Adam gleefully revealed to *Rolling Stone*. "I was so sick of typical lyrics like 'Ooh, baby' and 'I love you' and all this vague shit. I thought the more explicit I got without being totally explicit was a nice approach. The little girls would enjoy them and it would go right over my grandparents' heads, but it would hit my ex-girlfriend like a ton of bricks. It was perfect."

Unfortunately, MTV didn't think so, censoring all sexual references. "MTV has now edited the language," he exclaimed indignantly. "They won't let me say, 'Keep her coming every night' and they took the 'sinking' out of 'sinking my fingertips'. It's like fucking Communist China! It's totally bizarre."

Following the song's release to radio on January 27, 2004, an accompanying video took the opportunity to redress the balance. Directed by Sophie Muller, the woman responsible for Pink's 'Family Portrait', the video would feature Adam brazenly simulating sex with his new girlfriend – aspiring model Kelly McGee.

It had been increasingly difficult for Kelly – who would claim to see her boyfriend a maximum of one week a month – to watch him pour his heart out onstage each night in memory of his ex. Appearing in the video had been a way to restore her security and lend her some relevance to his professional life. The real-life object of his affections doubled as a fictional one as the two entwined themselves around each other, fully naked.

The public reaction – a hybrid of lust, disgust and hysteria – summed up the often vacuous celebrity culture that Adam had grown to despise. He'd always rejected the concept of fame without merit or for superficial reasons; yet in this case, that was exactly what had drawn listeners in. Proving more than ever the old adage that 'sex sells', it wrote the name 'Maroon 5' indelibly into the collective public consciousness.

The ensuing publicity brought the music to a wider audience – but Adam was totally bewildered by all the fuss. In any case, by his account it was nothing more than a simulation. "I didn't get horny or anything," he insisted, "which was weird since I shot it with my girlfriend."

Careful camera angles had ensured nothing more than intended was revealed. Yet MTV – along with the other major channels – struck again, acting quickly to censor the pair by smothering them in computer-generated flowers. Even with the additional modesty, *The Telegraph* tried its best to ignite the flames of scandal by crowning the video "porno-pop".

In an incredulous Mickey's eyes, it was "an absurd over-reaction". "Man, oh man, those digital flowers," he mocked. "Nudity and sexuality are not the problem – the problem is crass, empty and cheap pseudo-sexuality. We strive to be sincere in everything we do and sex is a big issue in our songs."

If Adam was initially enraged that his artistic expression – stemming from his genuine feelings towards Jane – had been censored, he didn't show it. "I don't care," he responded. "The kids know what I'm saying anyway. It's just a little sexuality – if that scares people, that's a shame. There's a lot left to the imagination. It's amazing that adults are so much sicker than kids are."

Another obstacle for Adam to negotiate was the tendency of the public to fit artists into two categories: either sex symbols whose main purpose was to provide visual pleasure, or serious artists who kept their flesh under wraps. Adam didn't mind being portrayed as an object of desire in the least, but his gripe was: why couldn't sex be taken seriously?

"It's because they're jealous," he evaluated mournfully. "If we were fake and ugly, we'd be critically acclaimed . . . because that whole sex symbol thing comes into it, it changes people's perceptions of our band. It's kind of an unfortunate by-product of the way we are marketed. We're starting to take more control of that. All those things will be altered and hopefully repaired by the time we make the next record."

In the meantime, gay magazine *The Advocate* had come to its own conclusion about Adam's motives for the video. "It's hard enough to lust over an unattainable celebrity without his simulating sex," the interviewer chastised. "Are you trying to torture fans – particularly gay men?"

"Yes," he shot back teasingly, without missing a beat. "The whole reason I started playing music was specifically to torture gay men."

In fact, as an incurable exhibitionist, Adam just thrived on pushing boundaries. "I don't want to just show a little bit of skin," he would explain to the *Miami Herald*. "I want to go for it."

He also lambasted Middle America's hysterical reaction to nakedness at the February 1 Superbowl performance featuring Justin Timberlake and Janet Jackson, where the former accidentally ripped his singing partner's costume down to reveal a breast disguised only by a substantial, star-shaped nipple piercing. Some opined that the stunt had been deliberate – after all, who regularly wore nipple piercings under their clothes for an event if they didn't intend on stripping down? – and argued it had been posed as an accident to avoid attracting hefty indecency fines.

The incident caused large-scale public condemnation, with parents threatening to boycott both acts in a wave of morally righteous indignation. Nervous industry bosses have been on high alert ever since.

"Her tit was hanging out [and] all of a sudden we were in the fifties again," Adam recalled incredulously. "I'm all about public displays of nudity, but if you're going to do it, don't do it that way . . . I wish they had gone further with it and done the song naked."

Of course, he had reached that milestone first, confessing, "I just love being as naked as possible all the time – it just feels really natural to me." He would also admit that, unlike his bandmates, he enjoyed being the centre of attention when making videos. "I love being in front of a camera," he affirmed. "It's fun. It's kind of like a weird fetish – it's exhilarating because I force myself to do it. It's kind of like masochistic behaviour."

And yet there was nothing painful about the song's reception – this was the track that would make Maroon 5 a big hit internationally. It reached the Top 10 in 12 countries, peaking at number three in the UK and number five in the US, even hitting the top spot in a sprinkling of other European territories.

By September 2004, the album would reach its stateside peak at number six – not bad for a CD that most reviewers had sneered at. As for the comparisons to Stevie Wonder, Adam regarded them as a compliment; in fact, he would cite Stevie's singing voice as the single biggest inspiration for the album.

Peaking a full 26 months after its initial release, *Songs About Jane* broke records for the longest gap between release and first appearance in the Top 10 since Soundscan had first started documenting it, well over a decade earlier.

Evidently, Ben Berkman had been right when he'd predicted it would be a slow burn. Yet it was worth the wait. Whereas Reprise had given up on Kara's Flowers after failing to see instant results, Octone had waited patiently for Maroon 5's baby steps to become adult strides – and now the label was celebrating a platinum album.

"With Maroon 5, we wouldn't have been satisfied to sell 150,000 albums of their debut release and move on," Ben explained. "We want to sell a million copies of a debut release – even if it takes two and a half years to do it."

By the end of 2004, they would more than fulfil that target, boasting a sales tally that exceeded three million. By this time, promotion was barely necessary – publicity in the preceding two years had generated so many followers that their live album, *1.22.03 Acoustic*, released in June, never made it higher than number 42 yet remained in the US chart long enough to sell over a million copies – with almost no marketing budget at all. With songs as varied as the Beatles' 'If I Fell', showcasing their sixties power-pop roots and AC/DC's 'Highway To Hell' bringing up the rock end, it showcased the diversity of Maroon 5 as a live band.

The same month, Adam's song 'Woman', described by MTV as a "sexy, sultry number" about obsession with a lover, made it onto the *Spider-man 2* soundtrack. "I remember very vividly writing that song," he recollected fondly. "I wrote it at my friend's room in some fancy hotel in New York where old people and business-people go. I remember I sat and was totally silent, which is rare for me, and like wrote these lyrics in about 10 minutes. I just spat them out and I never really changed them."

The other milestone that year was that, on their 10th anniversary as a band, *Songs About Jane* had gone platinum. This 2004 triumph corresponded with exactly the same day in 1994 when Mickey, Jesse, Adam and Ryan had started their journey as Kara's Flowers – something a deeply spiritual Jesse would no doubt describe as numerically meaningful synchronicity. The coincidence – or twist of fate – was a reminder of how arduous the road to success had been, of how hard they'd worked and how far they'd come.

Within a month of the acoustic CD hitting the shops – giving Maroon 5 two albums on the US chart concurrently – 'She Will Be Loved' was released as the third single. While there was a risk that so many successive releases would cannibalise sales for each newcomer on the market, 'She Will Be Loved' was a Top 5 hit in every English-speaking territory, even boasting a five-week run at number one in Australia. While 'This Love' had been their first truly successful single, with their follow-up they'd truly avoided the sophomore slump.

Following its July 27 release, the video became enormously popular on the music channels. Adam plays a man infatuated with his fiancee's mother, seeing her face every time he looks at her daughter. His mother-in-law-to-be is in an abusive relationship, suffering a husband who is both violent and emotionally unresponsive, leading Adam to watch uneasily when he slaps her in the face and to wish that he could offer her a better life.

To his delight, the heiress, model and socialite Kelly Preston, wife of movie star John Travolta, was cast as the object of his desires – the ultimate attractive older woman. On the day of the shoot, a petrified Adam would learn that pressure to perform wasn't just restricted to music. Worried that he might have early-morning halitosis, he had a constant supply of breath mints on hand for the kissing scenes with Kelly. However, all went well and he would loudly and publicly brag afterwards: "I got to make out with an older woman!"

After this undiplomatic display, he had the shock of his life when he came face to face with her real-life husband in the flesh. Primed for an altercation, he was surprised to find Travolta completely unmoved. "He said to me, 'If I was ever going to let anyone make out with my wife, it would be you!'" an incredulous Adam recalled. "I thought he was going to kick my ass, but he was totally cool!"

A far more awkward moment came when the tabloids seized upon flimsy evidence that he might have been having a fling with fellow vocalist Jessica Simpson – who just so happened to be married at the time – and emblazoned their suspicions across all the gossip columns. When it came to reporting rumours, sometimes being spotted chatting to someone at a party or even, often by pure coincidence, staying at the same hotel on the same night, equated with a full-blown affair.

Adam was especially sensitive about the allegations, as they arose at the time of the collapse of Jessica's relationship with her husband – and he was furious at being implicated as a marriage breaker. In addition, he rejected any association with the celebrity world she inhabited and that he, as an artist, seemed to have been automatically connected to. Widely regarded as a ditzy blonde, Jessica was, rightly or wrongly, better known for her good looks, flowing locks and dream body than for any contribution to music. Whether she was truly capitalising on her looks to gain fame and disguise a lack of musical credentials, or whether she was the victim of a shallow society that valued physical appearance over talent, was debatable. After all, Adam himself had complained bitterly of experiencing such prejudice after the raunchy video aired for 'This Love'.

Adam had argued that good looks shouldn't be a barrier to an artist – no matter how much a vocalist chose to flaunt it. Perhaps he had more in common with Jessica than the layperson might think. She embodied the archetypal male fantasy – as did Paris Hilton – but Adam felt compelled to deny he'd slept with either, so adamantly was he against the cult of celebrity.

He'd built up a casual friendship with Paris which had come to light after her mobile phone was hacked and the celebrity-studded contents of her address book made public – but there had been no amorous intentions. In fact, he was keen to distance himself as far as he possibly could from the concept of fame for its own sake.

"I'm not Paris Hilton," he would declare. "I'm not somebody that yearns for the public's attention so much that I perpetuate it. There are stars who base their whole existence on going to parties . . . It used to be that you were famous for a reason – for being an actor, a musician, a philanthropist, or a president. Now somebody can be famous for being a slut. It's just so boring. At the end of the day you don't want to be known for something stupid that you could end up regretting for the rest of your life. So [for me] there will be no sex tapes. There will be no reality television."

Adam's words may have seemed controversial – after all, one view was that a teenage Paris may have been manipulated into appearing in the sex tapes that shot her to notoriety and had never intended for such a private possession to go public. Plus, as a wealthy heiress who was already well-known on the showbiz circuit, she had little reason to pursue fortune and fame. Moreover, as someone who would later admit to the accuracy of reports that depicted him as a womaniser – defending his status on the grounds that he loved the fairer sex so much – was Adam not being rather hypocritical when he branded others 'sluts'?

Sexual politics aside, the merits of his argument about those who became famous for no good reason was obvious. Sex tapes were too numerous to be assigned much cultural value and the 'stars' were rarely seen as talented outside of the bed sheets.

The unsettling irony was that, while the artists, philanthropists and politicians of whom Adam spoke may have been making tangible efforts to change their world, they received far less press than the relationship status of Nicole Richie or the weight-loss plan of Kim Kardashian – according to the tabloids, these socialites were far worthier candidates for public attention. It was for this reason – and, of course, his desire to avoid the same stereotypes – that he would abstain from dating in the celebrity pool for several years.

In fact, following his short-lived romance with Kelly McGee, he had begun to see an anonymous cocktail waitress whose life was a picture of normality. For now, his private life was under wraps – and it would be staying that way.

Maroon 5, as a band, wanted to be known for something more meaningful than one-night stands – they wanted to be seen as creative musicians, political activists, even as instruments of peace. Most of all, they yearned for recognition in their own right, not as mere objects of desire.

After the 2004 presidential elections, Mickey made the group's aspirations to participate in the multi-faceted debate that was global politics abundantly clear. "So we've handed our country back to a bunch of Leo Strauss-worshipping social Darwinist, Christian fundamentalist homophobic hawks!" he exclaimed, clearly exasperated by the news that Republican President George W. Bush had been re-elected for a second term. "What a pathetic display from everyone involved . . . by the standards of any other age, the level of public discourse over the last year has been embarrassingly devoid of substance and intellect. We really have our media outlets to blame for the miserable failure of democracy that we're witnessing before our very eyes; their slavish devotion to their sponsors has effectively turned our brain into mush and this devotion just reflects the greater problem, which is the blur between public and private sectors and the almost complete takeover of public service by private interests. The so-called journalists in the mainstream news media who have been covering this administration should be beyond ashamed of themselves – they should hold themselves personally responsible for the myriad messes we're in!"

These words might have been seen as a little inflammatory. Fortunately for relations within the band, however, all five members held Democratic sympathies and were fiercely anti-Republican. Jesse would echo Mickey's confusion and sorrow that millions of his countrymen had voted Bush into government a second time running.

"How can we bring our country together?" he'd asked. "How can we . . . understand the motives of a majority of the voter population who supported the Bush administration? Evangelical Christians, conservatives, people who support the Republican tax policy, people who don't support same sex marriage – these are just some of the groups that helped re-elect the president and therefore these are some of the groups that he'll have to shape his policies for . . . what jumps into my head immediately is great sadness and shock."

There were numerous reasons why Jesse and his bandmates had rejected Bush. He had slashed taxes in a bid to speed up financial growth, but – in the views of certain leading economists – had caused a catastrophic increase in national debt instead. He'd also failed to act on an early warning about the 9/11 attacks, despite a report by the intelligence services that an 'event' was about to take place, feeding the suspicions of those who'd noted the neo-conservative claim that the USA 'needed' another Pearl Harbor to bring it together. Following the attacks, Bush then launched the War on Terror in retaliation – an action which Jesse strongly felt was heavy-handed:

"I feel like ever since the Bush administration released their official explanation for the attacks of September 11, the outrageously simplistic and misleading 'They hate us because we're a beacon of freedom,' the real truth about things has been buried in a glossy media presentation of a fake world," he mused.

One of Jesse's biggest issues with the War on Terror was that Bush had declared war on Iraq based on flimsy – and, as it later emerged, misleading – evidence. He'd vociferously claimed that Saddam Hussein's regime had to be defeated because they possessed weapons of mass destruction – which was later revealed to be untrue.

Yet if Bush had seemed cavalier in the face of these historical facts, the final straw for Jesse was his live-for-now attitude when it came to environmental policies. He'd declared that the Kyoto Protocol – aimed at hugely reducing greenhouse gases – was too expensive to fully implement and had made the controversial claim that, if global warming was a problem at all, it was not man-made. For Jesse, whose sister worked in the field of eco-friendly renewable energy and campaigned for better eco-policies, Bush's attitude was unsupportable.

Mickey's own sense of injustice was inflamed by the President's unconditional support of Israel. He felt so strongly about the rights of Palestinians that he'd even arrived at the Europe Music Awards clad in a pro-Palestine T-shirt, causing the public to criticise him for taking sides.

However, Mickey was resolute. "If it was 1944, I'd be wearing a shirt bearing the Israeli flag," he fought back. "I stand in solidarity with any displaced and disenfranchised people and my passion for a Palestinian state is motivated by a desire for peace, for both Israelis and Palestinians. I don't support the violence of Palestinian suicide bombers any more than I do the violence of the Israeli army as it bulldozes Palestinian homes and shoots women and children. I want this miserable cycle of suffering to end and I believe strongly that the answer is an immediate implementation of a free Palestinian state living alongside Israel. My statement of support for the struggle for Palestinian statehood was motivated only by a desire for a more peaceful and harmonious world for not only Jews and Arabs, but everyone."

For Ryan's part, he contributed to the political debate while on tour in London. Opening a copy of the *Daily Mirror*, he saw the condemnatory headline: "How could 59,000,000 people be so dumb?" Realising instantly that it referred to those who'd re-elected Bush, he took to the internet to publicly agree with every word.

The band had stood together both in their rejection of Bush and in their support of Democratic presidential candidate John Kerry. The latter had liberal views on homosexuality and social policy, and was strongly against criminalising abortion – all matters that Maroon 5 agreed on.

Jesse's sister had gifted him a mug that quipped, "If you're not outraged, then you're not paying attention" – and the group agreed. They aimed to use their public profiles to raise awareness and to encourage the world to pay attention.

"We don't deal with any political issues in our songs so they might write us off as another fluffy pop group," vented James. "That's fair if they don't know anything about us, but we do feel a responsibility now we're in this position to bring attention to issues that we feel are important."

They were bringing politics to those who might not formerly have taken notice. Determined to be socially aware, they were using their fame responsibly.

In contrast, Paris Hilton – desperate to claw her way back into the public's favour after a series of driving offences – had claimed she wanted to stop partying and to help African children. She would follow up this gesture by first confessing she thought the region was a country, not a continent.

Adam needn't have worried, after all. There was little chance of any member of Maroon 5 being compared to Paris or dismissed as a vacuous showbiz opportunist now.

6

Love Is The Greatest Drug

"WOULD I stand out in the pouring rain for a girl? Yes," Adam declared. "Any guy who would say no is a liar."

His lyrics were true to life then. Yet while he might have seemed like a romantic masochist, it had all paid off in the end. After all, as the end of the year 2004 approached, Maroon 5 had sold over three million copies of *Songs About Jane*. A CD that was originally born out of sorrow and agony at lost love had made him a millionaire. Songs he'd written not because he'd wanted to, but because he desperately needed an outlet for his frustration, were now known around the world.

What better way to taste emotional revenge? Better still for Adam, Jane was disapproving of what he'd done.

In a stroke of delight for his ego, when played live in concert those same songs had reduced some audience members to tears. "That's awesome!" he'd bragged to MTV. "That's so Michael Jackson. It really freaked me out. Who knows, maybe there was something in their eyes. That's what we want. I want our shows to have masses of sexuality and crying."

While Adam would state with hindsight that "having your heart stepped on is very common", the silver lining for him was turning pain into beauty in a way that – as evidenced by the crying – others could be moved by.

"Don't ever be afraid to fall in love," Adam would cheekily advise. "It may make you a very successful person at some point. If you can channel all that frustration, you never know what may happen."

Now that Maroon 5 were famous, what were they going to do with their fame? Remembering their commitment to social change rather than mere self-indulgence, by October 5, 2004, the band had made their first philanthropic gesture with the release of the compilation album *Mary Had A Little Amp*. Appearing alongside artists such as Madonna, REM and Moby, they reworked the song 'Pure Imagination' from *Willie Wonka & The Chocolate Factory*. The message promoted the cause of guaranteeing a preschool education for all American children.

Following that, 'Sunday Morning' was released as a single on December 4. For the promo video, they'd headed to the legendary Abbey Road Studios in London, where the Beatles had recorded most of their back catalogue and Pink Floyd had given birth to *The Dark Side Of The Moon*, for a simple but striking performance. Comically, they inserted a brief clip of a Japanese man singing 'This Love', karaoke-style, for the opening scene. They incorporated the scene in honour of their first ever visit to Japan, where they'd been tickled to find a few of their songs on the playlist at a karaoke bar.

While the single performed modestly this time around, it nonetheless charted in the Top 40 in every English-speaking country. In addition, 'Sunday Morning' already had an anthem–like status in the film world due to its appearance on the *Love Actually* and *Something's Gotta Give* soundtracks. When it debuted as a single, it attracted attention from the producers of a third film and, by 2005, was also featured in *Cheaper By The Dozen 2*.

Yet the one event that cemented Maroon 5's status as a household name was their appearance at the 2005 Grammy Awards. Not only did they help to open the show for a TV audience that reached into the millions, they also took home the Best New Artist award. At that time, controversial rapper Kanye West had just risen into the mainstream and Adam had been convinced that, of all the nominees, he was the only one with a fighting chance – so much so that he'd tapped Kanye on the shoulder to wryly assert, "Hey man, I think you got this one!"

He was wrong. "The actual moment they called our names was a total shock," Adam would recall with amazement. "I was in shock so much . . . I couldn't focus on anything and I felt kind of sick to my stomach. It was just a strange experience."

Time seemed to pass in slow motion for Adam as he imagined himself almost back at school. "All the award shows, they have strange vibes to them, kind of like a high school assembly where they're passing out awards to people in your class," he continued. "It's almost the same type of dynamic there – the cool kids, the punky kids and the jocks – all the different cliques there are in this world of music. We try and have a really good time at these things but it's hard to really get behind the idea that we're involved in them."

Even with the award in his hand, he found it difficult to process that he'd beaten off competition like Kanye West. "There was a lot of critical attention focused on him," Adam mused, "so naturally I think he probably thought he was going to win – and so did we, to be honest!"

Kanye took the loss surprisingly well. He didn't have a reputation as someone who accepted defeat gracefully – in fact, over the ensuing years he'd make a name for himself as quite the opposite. In 2006, he'd be outraged when his video for 'Touch The Sky' lost out to Justice and Simian's 'We Are Your Friends' for a coveted Europe Music Award and gave an expletive-loaded speech to express his disgust. "It cost a million dollars!" he exclaimed. "Pamela Anderson was in it! I was jumping across canyons! If I don't win, the awards show loses credibility!"

Subsequently, in 2007 he would vow "never to return" to MTV after Britney Spears was chosen to open the Video Music Awards instead of him, saying, "She hasn't had a hit record in years!" To add insult to injury, he then failed to win in any of the five categories for which he had been nominated. Backstage, he accused the show of racism, insisting, "Give a black man a chance!"

Yet the biggest faux pas of all was storming the stage in indignation when Taylor Swift won a VMA, arguing that rival nominee Beyoncé's 'Single Ladies (Put A Ring On It)' was "the best video of all time". Occasionally, Kanye would give a begrudging apology for his indiscretions before going on to repeat them all over again the next year.

While none of those outbursts predated the 2005 Grammys, there had been a similar episode at the 2004 American Music Awards, when his debut album, *The College Dropout*, lost out to country artist Gretchen Wilson. "I feel I was definitely robbed," he'd told an interviewer backstage in no uncertain terms. "I refuse to give any politically correct bullshit ass comment. *I* was the Best New Artist this year."

Accepting that he hadn't been voted top dog in any given event was a desperate struggle for Kanye, which made his burgeoning friendship with

Adam – and restraint when he lost out to him for an award – all the more surprising. In fact, the Grammys would bring the pair together for a collaboration. They had history already – it had been Adam's dream, since attending Five Towns College, to see his work reinterpreted by a hip-hop producer and, as one of his "favourite musicians", Kanye had been number one on the shortlist.

Thus piano extraordinaire John Legend – who'd played on Jay-Z's and Alicia Keys' albums to name but a few – had teamed up with Kanye to create a Stevie Wonder and gospel-inspired remake of 'This Love'. Literally shaking with excitement at the new sound, Maroon 5 had hotly debated releasing it to urban radio – or, at the very least, the mix-tape market. However, it had lost its expected hip-hop element, leaving them hesitant about where it might fit. "It ended up being more like a track from Stevie Wonder's *Songs In The Key Of Life* than a hip-hop track," Adam would later acknowledge, "so we didn't put it out."

Yet there remained a strong respect between himself and Kanye. The pair soon caught up with one another on a flight to Rome, during which the rapper was showing off work in progress for his forthcoming album. "He started playing me stuff on his iPod – all his new material for his record – and I was really excited about it," Adam recalled. "Then he played me this song ['Heard 'Em Say']. He was rhyming over it and I had just written a hook that was perfect for it!"

Adam felt a rush of desperation to be included in the song. However, Kanye would take some convincing – not least because he felt that Maroon 5's mainstream popularity might compromise Adam's street cred. "I had to fight with myself because he's so good, yet he's so popular," Kanye would explain. "The popularity takes away from the illness of having him."

Still, he had the nagging suspicion that the blending of each singer's musical styles might just make the difference between a good song and a great one – or a commercially successful one and a flop. So far he'd played the skeleton of the track to as many girls as he could find, hoping for their approval, but when it came it was muted. Meanwhile, Adam was concerned that the hook he'd devised might not appeal to Maroon 5 fans because it was "too R&B". Mixed with Kanye's rap track however, it might turn the tables for both of them.

Yet Kanye had been deliberating, unsure of himself – until the moment he overheard Adam's voice at the Grammy rehearsals. Taken aback, he exclaimed: "Adam's so ill! His voice sounds like a fucking instrument. The only other dude that has a voice like that is Akon." It sealed the deal for him – his Grammy awards rival would be on the track.

One quality that Adam loved about Kanye, which he felt was sorely lacking in most of his rap contemporaries, was his tendency to pack a political punch. Some rappers would repeatedly rhyme about topless models, Cristal champagne, obscenely expensive cars and the more superficial aspects of showbiz, glamorising a lifestyle that was materialistic, wasteful or sometimes immoral. To Adam, that was wasting an opportunity to inspire social change. If the whole world was listening, why not hold up a mirror to society's weak spots and encourage millions to do the same? In contrast, bragging about a diamond-encrusted Lamborghini seemed ultimately meaningless. Yet Kanye was using his platform for good causes, underlining that he and Adam had something significant in common.

'Heard 'Em Say' quickly developed into a song written from the perspective of an impoverished American citizen at the mercy of a ruthless, unfeeling government. The track touched upon atrocities that had taken place in the false name of religion, while bemoaning a minimum wage that left many low-income workers living on the breadline. It was particularly socially insightful for someone already on the path to creating a lucrative empire, who might otherwise be expected to be dazzled by the trappings of fame.

The most darkly controversial part of the song was Kanye's allegation that he knew the government had deliberately "administered AIDS". For some listeners this might have seemed far-fetched, perhaps a political statement too far. Yet in Kanye's defence, the track was urging people to "be honest with yourself in a world that is not" and he'd done just that by expressing his unorthodox belief.

The track was Adam's first major project away from his bandmates. Once it was recorded, Maroon 5 moved on to their first headlining arena tour, which would take them across America. Sponsored by Honda Civic, it seemed to go against their political instincts – in fact, James had admitted to being "wary of doing any sort of corporate sponsorship".

But in this case it was different. The Japanese car manufacturer matched their environmental policies and the Civic was an eco-friendly, fuel-efficient model. "The interesting hook wasn't necessarily ticket sales with them," Honda senior manager Tom Peyton guessed correctly. "I think they are in a position, with their notoriety, to put forth some good causes. Certainly the whole ecology situation is one they feel strongly about."

In honour of the collaboration, the band even designed a special edition Honda with a "sick sound system" and "tripped-out *Pimp My Ride* sort of wheels". The sleek white hybrid car – complete with an enormous Maroon 5 crest on the front, flanked by lions on each side – even came with its own iPod and would accompany the band during the entire two-month tour. Meanwhile, ticket holders could compete to win their own Maroon 5-customised cars.

Due to its energy-efficient status, having their own personalised car came with guilt-free bragging rights. The shiny designer model high-lighted just how fast their careers had accelerated – from the stench of urine in a tiny, barely functional van to the scent of brand new leather and their own customised wheels.

Yet a car wasn't all the group had designed – as part of the package, they'd also produced a website with information on energy efficiency, tailored to raise awareness among music fans and offering facts such as: "Did you know you could run a TV set for three years with the energy saved from recycling an aluminium can?"

"It's so rare," James marvelled, "to sign on for the marketing of a product that can actually change the world."

The adventure with Maroon 5 would be Honda's fifth annual music tour, and the first that did not feature predominantly rock acts. In previous years they'd taken the likes of Blink 182, Sum 41, Incubus, Good Charlotte, Linkin Park and New Found Glory on the road, whereas the collaboration with Maroon 5 marked a subtle change in direction. In fact, in the following year they would stretch their boundaries even further with a tour featuring the Black Eyed Peas and Pussycat Dolls.

Meanwhile, Maroon 5 looked set to make their two-month stint an eventful one. They'd blend old favourites with a motley crew of covers ranging from Pink Floyd's 'Another Brick In The Wall' to Sting's 'Message In A Bottle' and a jazzy makeover of the Police's 'Roxanne'.

Joining them on their musical mystery tour were Phantom Planet, Irish rock band the Thrills, old friends from back home in California, and the Donnas – an all-girl group with colourful personalities and audacious anthems such as '40 Boys In 40 Nights', controversially chronicling a lustful tour full of one-night stands. Whether any of the Maroon 5 boys became notches on their bedposts remains unknown but, in a cheeky nod to the Donnas' predilection for the male of the species, the headliners arranged for them to be confronted by strippers dressed as policemen. Meanwhile, Donnas drummer Torry Castellano returned the favour by providing background vocals on 'This Love'.

Rolling Stone had formerly described the Donnas as "a good old-fashioned rock'n'roll party" – and if that's what Maroon 5 had expected, they wouldn't be disappointed. As Mickey would later state, "We were very sad to see the Donnas go."

The Donnas episode wasn't the only encounter with strippers on the tour – the female variety offered entertainment too. "They were all over us, bumping and grinding in their G-strings," Mickey recalled after their support act had returned the favour. "They threw us all around and even kicked us. We were still shaking when we got onstage."

Adam was already well-acquainted with exotic dancers, having seen his first at a recording studio while still a teenager, but for the others – especially James, whose internal war between treading a conservative Mormon path and following his desires waged on – it was their first experience.

The same night, Mickey would shock his bandmates by breaking into an impromptu rendition of 'This Love' onstage, without forewarning. "My band always says I have the voice of an angel," he recalled with smug satisfaction, "so [secretly] I picked up the mike that their monitor guy uses to talk to them in their 'in-ears' during the show and had him turn it up really loud. I sang at the top of my lungs and I think I did a great job. When I started singing, all the guys looked over to see who could be making such a sound. I think I really impressed them!"

Meanwhile, to keep themselves entertained between shows, the band had been listening to historical anecdotes of the legendary tours through-out rock history. "Our first tour manager once described life on the road like a cross between outer space and the Wild West," Mickey quipped, "and he's a man who knows – although it's not as crazy nowadays as it was in 1969."

He was referring to the infamous events that unfolded in a documentary about the Rolling Stones that the band had watched avidly, called *Gimme Shelter*. Taking its name from a Stones song, the film centred on their ill-fated Altamont Speedway concert near Oakland in California – an event said by one reviewer to have "actively stamped out the last stretch of sixties utopia". It did so by demonstrating what could happen if the public were 'policed' by a self-proclaimed outlaw gang, instead of by professionals.

A free-for-all for 300,000 people, the free concert had quickly spiralled out of control. The Hells Angels had been placed in charge of security, but – armed with pool cues and knives – they were ready to fight anyone who challenged their authority. They set about beating troublesome spectators, eventually stabbing one reveller to death (though the young man was brandishing a handgun).

Watching the documentary had originally been a means of warding off boredom during a 12-hour drive to Miami, but the group quickly found themselves enthralled. "Not a good vibe for a concert," Mickey would sympathise. "Guns and stabbing and too many people taking too many drugs. Just making it through the movie made me feel like we got through something together!"

Back in the cold light of reality, the Maroon 5 tours seemed about as edgy as a pensioner's outing to a bingo hall in comparison to the Stones' antics both on and offstage. "I ruined Adam's room with a tube of Pringles that exploded everywhere," James recalled, "[but] I realise that doesn't sound very rock'n'roll. I don't see exploding Pringles being a highlight of the Rolling Stones or Led Zeppelin after parties!"

With that said, Maroon 5 had their fair share of hedonism backstage, with Primal Scream blaring out of the speakers as a backdrop. On one occasion, the group were smoking marijuana, only to be accosted by policemen and caught red-handed. Yet it didn't end quite as they had expected.

"Two policemen came in and asked us what we were up to," Mickey recalled. "The room got really silent and I felt like I was having a heart attack. The cops kept questioning me for a while and then one of them took the 'cigarette' out of one of the guys' hands and took a hit . . . and then the music started!"

Yet while all those moments would take pride of place in the group's memory banks, they'd learnt to put a little water in their wine and temper the fun with self-restraint. They were aware of the downfall of stars like Jimi Hendrix and Jim Morrison – brightly burning talents extinguished by the magnetising draw of substance abuse – and knew that if they didn't apply the brakes, they risked losing everything they'd worked to achieve.

"I've written some of the best music ever stoned!" Adam would later confess. "But I've also written some truly horrible music. Anything beyond that recreational use of drugs is terrifying.

"What upsets me is this romantic new look at sex, drugs and rock'n' roll," he added. "The allure of it is incredible. Drugs must have seemed amazing in the sixties, but . . . we need a modern outlook. This idea that rock'n'roll has to be this way is archaic. Perpetuating it as this mythical thing that you have to live up to is so stupid. Back in the days when the Beatles were on acid, they were writing fucking *Sgt Pepper*. There was something happening culturally that was a phenomenon. Now it's just the acid and no *Sgt. Pepper*!"

Adam made no secret of his fondness for soft drugs, yet he would take a considered step back from anything too self-destructive. Consequently, life on tour fluctuated from one extreme to another – from marijuana to meditation.

For their part, Jesse and James had begun to attend meditation classes on the road. "It was such a powerful experience," Jesse shared afterwards. "It was like a waking dream. The way time passed was so strange – 40 minutes flew by in what seemed like 10 minutes [while] sometimes 10 minutes feels like it takes an hour to go by. There is this infinite world to tap into and it feels so good!"

Centring himself this way countered the stress of the tour, which saw dozens of cities fly by in an equal number of days. It lowered the risk that, when weak and vulnerable and isolated from those he loved back home, he might seek solace via toxic methods.

One of the lessons Jesse had attended had a profound effect on him when his tutor spoke of the power of mind over matter and the possibility of transforming physical pain. Using a meditation technique, she'd cured herself of a headache.

"She was able to pay close attention to the sensation of pain and discomfort in her head and then imagine the exact opposite sensation, willing her body to experience that state of bliss, if only in her imagination – but the imagination is a very powerful thing," Jesse recalled. "It is in many ways responsible for everything we think we know."

The impact of the human mind over the body had been the topic of much research in both the scientific and spiritual fields over the years. Both disciplines – despite how different they were – saw evidence of the phenomenon. For example, the so-called 'placebo effect' is believed to occur when a patient is administered a treatment for a pain or ailment and perceives him or herself to have been cured as a result, even when in reality they have received a sugar pill with no medicinal value. The theory is that because the patient believes they have been cured, they achieve a state of mind positive enough to counteract – or at least neutralise – the original problem.

There are scientifically sound and medically accepted explanations for the placebo effect and of course meditation – for example, stress is known to weaken the immune system, while positive thinking releases 'happy' chemicals known as endorphins into the bloodstream to mitigate any negative physical sensations, hence the old adage 'laughter is the best medicine'. Exercise is known to produce an endorphin-infused adrenalin rush too, explaining why marathon runners and professional sportsmen and women are often able to display extreme endurance in spite of severe injury.

A similar effect may also be observed in the case of emotional trauma. Disassociation occurs as a means of 'zoning out' and visualising oneself somewhere else as an escape from physical or mental distress. The spiritual camp believes this is about learning to separate the soul from the body and not allowing the latter to manipulate the patient's well-being.

"[Our teacher] has had a lot of practice with overcoming the idea that we are a slave to our bodies," Jesse explained, "and so she was able to imagine the state of bliss so clearly that she then simply had a choice – she could either remain in the painful state of the headache-afflicted body, or she could play around in the blissful state of the ecstatic body. Clearly, she chose what anyone would and was freed from discomfort for the rest of the day."

However, back in the Maroon 5 camp, some physical pain was so sharp that no amount of meditation could hope to heal it. Up until the previous year, the group had been afflicted by nothing more threatening than the niggling irritation of impacted wisdom teeth. James would joke that, while his contorted face onstage may have given fans the impression that he was "intensely focused in musical ecstasy", he was actually in "intense pain".

As agonising as the sensation was, the solution was simple – to have them removed. It hadn't disrupted a single show, but more recently there'd been two exceptions to that rule. The least threatening of the two was an injury sustained by Adam on the Honda tour, while he was toning his abs.

"He was working out with an elastic strap that you stick in the top of the door and pull down towards your chest," Jesse recounted. "It was fixed to the top of the door with a metal hook and the door was locked from the inside, but as it turns out the lock was broken. James opened the door just as Adam was pulling down on the strap with all his weight, so the metal hook slammed into his chest, splitting open a deep cut and fracturing his sternum. Adam was in shock because of the impact and because his entire shirt quickly became drenched in blood."

He was rushed to hospital in an ambulance, whereupon a worried doctor informed him it might be necessary to perform surgery. Fortunately, X-rays revealed that the damage incurred would heal by itself and, much to the astonishment of his bandmates, he was back onstage in Dallas the very same night, high on a cocktail of potent painkillers.

Ryan, on the other hand, wasn't so lucky. For a long time he'd been struggling in silence with acute pain in his shoulders and wrists, which also seemed to inflame every muscle and tendon in between. This was an agony so intense that no amount of meditation could have touched it.

Spurred on by Octone, the band had been touring constantly in support of *Songs About Jane* by the time Ryan suffered his first major meltdown. Describing himself as already "utterly exhausted and jet-lagged to an unreasonable degree", he'd been desperate for a break but, as their popularity increased, the schedule had merely become ever more gruelling. A continuous stream of TV appearances and CD signings in between shows merely accentuated the problem, leaving him no time to rest or recover.

Things would eventually come to a dramatic head after a three-night run at the House of Blues. "My right arm was shaking so hard. I was incapable of signing my own autograph," Ryan grimaced in memory of the episode. "I deteriorated to such a degree that both of my arms were pretty much useless."

At first the band had remained upbeat, believing it was merely a matter of tendon strain or pulled muscles and that restoring Ryan to full functioning was just a matter of securing the right medical treatment. Yet even after a week's rest at home – during which former Square member Ryland Steen stood in for him – he failed to show much improvement. He was fast losing coordination, even to the extent of his grip on the drumsticks. He struggled to maintain rhythm, due to the weakness and tremors in his muscles, and by this point no amount of painkilling medication was sufficient to ward off the near intolerable spasms.

In their drive to make Maroon 5 a big hit internationally, the band's management had continued to add more and more locations to their itinerary, leading to schedules that were continually revised to make way for additional concerts. At a Milanese airport, after seeing how an implausibly tight schedule would mean forfeiting a break they'd earlier been promised, Ryan couldn't hold back the frustration.

"I broke down," he recalled. "I saw another break evaporate and I could barely function. I knew I was near the end and it wouldn't be long before my grip would fail."

Despite taking further time off, with session duties fulfilled by fellow drummer Josh Day, and undergoing "every kind of exam and therapy imaginable", no one in the medical profession seemed to have any answers. "No-one could get a firm grip on what had gone wrong and how it could be resolved," Ryan recalled. "All I knew is that I couldn't play the drums."

This produced the terrifying realisation that he might *never* recover – something he hadn't dared to contemplate before. "Every show was a rush of adrenalin and pain, excitement and agony," he later reflected. "I lived with the daily anguish of knowing that it was just a matter of time before my body would give out on me." With specialists clueless as to why his arms had so dramatically crumbled, he had no choice but to continue as best he could – albeit with sporadic absences – and hope for a miracle.

Meanwhile, the group's fifth and final single from *Songs About Jane* hit the shops: 'Must Get Out'. The timing was apt, as the emotions expressed in the lyrics conveyed exactly the desperation a panicked Ryan had been enduring, as he yearned for a break from the tour to rest and recuperate. Unfortunately, to add to the group's overall despondency, it became their worst performing single to date; it barely scraped the Top 40 in the UK and its best chart position was the number eight spot in the Netherlands. Although it might have seemed as though their popularity was fading, it was usual for sales to peter out when it came to the final single, by the time that the marketing budget for the album had dwindled. In any case it would soon be time to hit the studio, although there were several more months of riding the wave yet to come.

On June 9, 2005, the boys were invited to perform at a tribute to legendary filmmaker George Lucas, best known for his creation of the *Star Wars* series. He was so well regarded in the industry that, unusually, the tribute event was taking place well before his death, when he was still active. In fact, Lucas had personally selected Maroon 5 to appear on the advice of his children, who considered the group their favourite.

The following month, another major event lay in store. Up until then, Adam had been insane with jealousy that his ex-girlfriend, Kelly McGee, had met Stevie Wonder at a charity event. As his idol played the hit 'Higher Ground', Adam had been forced to listen through a crackly phone line, at the mercy of his girlfriend's patchy mobile reception. It didn't much help that he had a competitive nature – from that moment onwards, he'd vowed to meet Stevie in person himself.

"I'm really bummed that I missed him," Adam had lamented, adding, "If Stevie Wonder knows who I am . . . knows of our music, I will know I've made it!"

He didn't have to wait long – that moment came courtesy of Bob Geldof's Live 8 charity event, aimed at raising awareness of endemic poverty in Africa. Geldof was calling for the debt of Third World countries to be cancelled, using popular groups as bait to coax those who would otherwise have ignored political issues.

On July 2, Maroon 5 appeared on the Philadephia stage in the company of artists like the Black Eyed Peas, who performed 'Get Up, Stand Up' with Rita and Stephen Marley – the ultimate protest song. During their own set, Maroon 5 offered a cover of Neil Young's 'Rockin' In The Free World' – an equally political, albeit more disillusioned, number. Then Adam took to the stage on his own, teaming up with closing act Stevie

Wonder for a dramatic finale – a joint rendition of the latter's 1970 hit 'Signed, Sealed, Delivered'. Barely able to conceal his awe, a beaming Adam grasped the hand of his idol – his wish had finally been achieved.

The event also provided yet another profound awakening for Jesse, who felt that the group's fans were united in a common cause. "The energy from the crowd was really different from what we've seen in the past," he mused. "I could feel in the way that people were dancing and singing that there was something more than just the appreciation of music in the air. I think it was the idea that everyone there was taking part in an event that was trying to improve the quality of life for suffering people. It's a beautiful concept. And it's hard to know exactly what can be done to support the hardships that people are undergoing all over the world, but it seems easy to support the idea of erasing the debt for the incredibly poor nations that obviously need to feed their people more than they need to repay debts to wealthy nations such as the United States."

The date of a G8 summit was approaching, where a group of major world leaders – including the much-loathed President Bush – would gather to discuss exactly how to ease such poverty. Feeling that Maroon 5's fans were a force to be reckoned with, as long as everyone's energy was focused on the same goal, Jesse issued a public plea for his followers to apply moral pressure on the President.

"Bush spoke a lot during his campaign about the fact that he is a compassionate conservative," he chided sarcastically, "and currently we're fighting a war in a country supposedly so that we can spread the joys of freedom and democracy to Iraq. So if our President is that concerned with people living free, then he'd better do everything in his power to help lift the burden of poverty from these starving nations."

In spite of the increasingly spiritual Jesse's urges for the public to "send out good vibrations", the outcome of the G8 summit was a disappointment – in the eyes of many, the meeting had held no serious intent and had been little more than a token gesture to the public. Yet Bob Geldof vowed that there would be another charity concert in the future and campaigners like Jesse would not be defeated.

Meanwhile, the Maroon 5 tour played on. In August, the summer season continued with an invitation to perform at their biggest UK show yet: Chelmsford's V Festival. The boys considered themselves committed

Anglophiles, boasting an enormous Britpop collection, and even claimed that the best music ever to be made hailed from the UK – all of which boded well for their visit. That said, not everyone reciprocated their love. Noel Gallagher, of ultimate Britpop kings Oasis, made his feelings only too clear: "If we had a hand at picking the bill, Maroon 5 wouldn't be on it."

Adding that, their unwanted intrusion aside, the line-up consisted exclusively of his friends, Noel tied the invisible velvet rope even tighter around the event. But then this type of banter was expected of the Gallagher brothers – they were notoriously outspoken, contemptuous of airs and graces and saw nothing wrong with revealing exactly how they felt, regardless of how difficult it was to swallow.

Yet for Adam, whether Noel adored or despised them, even to be acknowledged by one of Britain's most successful groups was a coup in itself. "The most flattering thing you can get, being an American band coming to England, is something from Oasis!" he insisted. "So thank you Noel for hating me – you've validated my existence!"

Later that month, there was another encounter with British rock royalty when Maroon 5 opened for the Rolling Stones. While they supported them stateside – in Hartford, Connecticut and Detroit – Adam was boasting his boundary-defying musical diversity again by appearing on a rap track from Atlanta-based hip-hop duo Ying Yang Twins.

Despite teaming up with Britney Spears, singing 'I Got That (Boom Boom)' for her album *In The Zone* and collaborating with Lil Jon on his single 'Get Low', the twins had never truly conquered the charts or become a household name. Yet Adam was instantly supportive of their song 'Live Again' as, like his work with Kanye West, it packed a political punch.

The duo shared the same background with many of those they were singing for: battling poverty, racism and depression in the USA's often discriminatory Deep South. They spoke of those born into the world without a concept of the hardship that lay ahead, claiming also that teachers had passed the buck to preachers – in their eyes, hypocrites who were unfit for the role – and all had left life's lessons to be passed down by the rappers.

'Live Again' was the controversial story of the life of a reluctant stripper.

The fictional woman became an orphan at eight years old and was reduced to a life of tearful shifts at strip clubs to pay her way through college. Already a mother with an unsupportive, unemployed partner, she also has to pay the rent and provide for her child. The lyrics adamantly claim she "ain't a ho", but is doing what she has to do purely to get by.

Adam sang the hook, questioning whether the demeaning lifestyle she lives will ever end. Intended to hold up a mirror to the struggles of society, the track was never released as a single but the album on which it appeared, *U.nited S.tate Of A.tlanta*, would go on to sell over a million copies.

As tour commitments to promote *Songs About Jane* gradually wound down, Adam's side projects had the space to accelerate. After promoting the live album *Friday The 13th*, which consisted of concert recordings from their 2005 arena tour, he would collaborate with soul songstress Alicia Keys on a cover of the Rolling Stones track 'Wild Horses'. For their collaboration, the two genre-defying artists teamed up at Alicia's concert at the Brooklyn Academy of Music in New York, and the results – which also included a rendition of 'Welcome To Jamrock' with Damian Marley – were recorded on her *Unplugged* album, which hit stores on October 7, 2005.

That same month, Adam and Kanye would appear together on *Saturday Night Live* for a performance of 'Heard 'Em Say'. In preparation for releasing the track as a single, the pair would also make a promotional video. Directed by Michel Gondry, who had previously reinvented the White Stripes as Lego figures, it would see Adam step into the less glamorous profession of a security guard at department store Macy's, giving access to Kanye and his three children after it closes.

"It's kind of a surrealistic Christmas world that Macy's becomes," Adam explained. "I let Kanye and his family in after hours to spend the night. He's got three kids with him and they're running around and I'm chasing them."

Genuinely filmed in the New York flagship store after close of business hours, it depicted objects and toys coming to life – just as Adam had visualised back in the Kara's Flowers days – and included scenes of a sofa bed folding and unfolding in time to the beat.

"There's this one scene where we're driving like a police car bed!" an amused Adam continued. "It's so weird. There's dancing suits in the men's section, all kinds of craziness! That was an experience culturally . . . it's inspirational to push yourself past what you're used to. It's nice to be a little bit uncomfortable if it can yield more interesting, unique results." The single made its debut on November 8, enhancing Adam's reputation in the rap camp and solidifying his status as a crossover artist.

★ ★ ★

Meanwhile, Jesse was renewing his interest in all things esoteric and spiritual. First he added *The Celestine Prophecy* to his bookshelf, which he would describe as "the *Da Vinci Code* of spiritual texts". "It's all about the last 10,000 years of human evolution – not physically, but emotionally and spiritually," he explained.

Then he found another book, *Mutant Message Down Under*, which chronicled the adventures of an American doctor who moves to Australia to work with native Aboriginals, only to get "quasi-kidnapped and taken on a walkabout in the harsh outback by a benevolent tribe".

The true-life story appealed to Jesse because it was the antithesis of the fast-paced Western world he inhabited. The tribe's back-to-basics living, free from technology or material trappings, established a focus on human interaction, spirituality and traditional customs and superstitions.

"The tribe communicates telepathically. They survive off the barest rations of food and water and they live in complete harmony with each other – the animals, the plants, the entire planet," he mused, before adding in mock incredulity, "They only have dial-up internet service – NO DSL!"

In contrast, every part of Jesse's life relied on communication technology: from the in-ear monitors onstage that allowed wireless transmission of the backing track to the mobile phone that seemed permanently glued to his ear on tour, his only link to the outside world. His whole life played itself out through a series of emails and text messages. His career depended on them, and yet he found the notion of a simpler life irresistible.

"Beyond their beautiful philosophy about sharing the earth with everything that lives and dies on it are the episodes where they heal injured members of the tribe," Jesse continued. "At one point a man falls down a hill and shatters his calf bone – and I mean the bone was sticking out of the skin – and the tribe leaders gather around him to first communicate with the bone and encourage it to become one with the body again. They move their hands about two inches above his skin, chanting and praying – and then after some time, they scream and the bone slides back into the skin. Then they put some homemade tar made from fermented human blood into the wound, they wrap him up, he goes to sleep, the next day he's ready to walk with the tribe again!"

Returning to the idea of mind over matter and the body's ability to heal itself, he added, "There's just no limit to what is possible, except for what we've been taught to believe."

As the weeks passed, Jesse pondered a further series of spiritual questions: Could people communicate with the dead? Was it possible to predict the future? Did having a simple life and fewer possessions set a person free when all else had failed?

He also began to explore the Buddhist philosophy of Zen, including the belief that the key to achieving something was to visualise it; imagining a desired outcome was said to create sufficient energy to set the wheels in motion for it to take place. Jesse had already been exploring the concept on a smaller scale with pain-healing meditation, but saw freeing Ryan from his pain with the power of Zen as the next step – an attempt which ultimately proved unsuccessful. He was also interested in attuning his energy to harmonise himself with the universe, working from the belief that the Earth vibrated at a specific energy frequency and humans had evolved over the centuries to respond best to that frequency. However, manmade technology and modern living could disrupt this delicate energy balance between human and environment, causing disharmony which could manifest itself as physical illness. For example, the frequency of a mobile phone when on a call is measured at millions of hertz faster than that of the Earth, and indeed of the human body. Some held wireless technology responsible for ailments as serious as cancer; while some dismissed the theory as ludicrous, it was supported by at least some medical research.

Jesse was also keen to study ancient customs and cultures, to see if they could have a positive impact when applied to the USA. Inspired by *Being Peace*, a book by Vietnamese Buddhist monk Thich Nhat Hanh, he even began to organise "a worldwide free trial of a day of peace".

"How nice would it be if everyone agreed that for one day they would try out total peace?" he asked. "Everyone would know that for 24 hours, no-one was going to harm them in any way. People in war zones could walk out into the street and have a picnic, play cards, dance, exercise, sunbathe, read, take a nap on the sidewalk, talk to anyone they met. We could start having this day of peace once a month. Maybe people would really enjoy it and want to try it once every week. Who knows where it could lead? I know it sounds crazy, but it could happen every day. You remember the John Lennon and Yoko Ono song – 'All we are saying is give peace a chance.' Think about it. It's never been given a chance all around the world – not even for one day."

Yet while Jesse was meditating his way to a vision of world peace, darker forces were plaguing the group. Ryan's percussion-related pains had become so severe that, as the *Songs About Jane* tour drew to a close, he felt he had no choice but to resign from the band altogether. His diagnosis had ranged from tendonitis to a trapped nerve, but for some time, his specialists had been forced to admit they'd run out of ideas. Facing an untreatable injury that seemed to have no hope of full recovery, by September 2006 he'd gathered his bandmates together to deliver the bad news.

Initially, the others were inconsolable. They'd gone into the band as brothers and, after over a decade together, had developed connections that felt as real as a blood bond. How could they continue without him?

"It was the most difficult thing," Adam admitted. "Me, Mickey, Ryan and Jesse would sleep on his bedroom floor and dream about how we were going to be the biggest band in the world someday."

In the view of their fans, this is exactly what had happened – but they couldn't move forwards together. With reluctance, they approached session musician Matt Flynn, who'd filled in for Ryan before during one of his many absences. With a CV that included work with the B-52s and Maroon 5 tourmate Gavin DeGraw, he seemed the ideal replacement.

That month, Ryan wrote an official statement of resignation on the group's Myspace page: "Due to the rigours of touring, I have sustained joint and nerve injuries that have made me unable to continue performing as a drummer in a touring rock band. I am therefore leaving Maroon 5 to pursue songwriting and producing on my own, a process I have already begun with much enthusiasm. The split is amicable and I have made my peace with this unfortunate reality because I feel that I have a lot of music still left to make."

Of course, in spite of his online bravado, there was still a raw tinge of disappointment in his heart. "There we were, enjoying ever more success, achieving unbelievable things," he later reflected, "and I was on my way home."

7

Running For The Hollywood Hills

WHILE a defeated Ryan was on his way home, Adam made the realisation that he didn't have one of his own to go to. Since the release of *Songs About Jane*, he had only been back to LA fleetingly, but, now that he had a gap in his schedule, he found himself in the unusual position of being simultaneously a multiplatinum-selling millionaire and homeless. "I suddenly had a career," he'd tell *Architectural Digest,* "but nowhere to live."

He soon solved the problem by snatching up a secluded forties hilltop bachelor pad, within eyeshot of the iconic Hollywood sign. By now tiring of the celebrity crowd, he was looking for a hideaway from where he could "survey his kingdom" without being spotted himself – and the ranch-style home perched atop Bronson Canyon was a real-life version of the ideal home sketched in his mind's eye. "I fell in love with the location and the privacy and the fact that it was such a low-key place," Adam explained. "It was Hollywood without being 'Hollywood'."

Now safe from the prying eyes of the public – not to mention the scrutiny of the media microscope – Adam set about renovating his dream property. Firstly, he had all of the upstairs walls removed, transforming four large bedrooms into one monumental one. Then, enlisting the help of his friend Mark Haddawy – co-owner of vintage fashion boutique Resurrection and keen collector of 20th-century art – he set about decorating it.

"Furnishing a home is no different than going into the studio and making music," described Adam. "You want to make sure you've pared down the extra details so that in the end, every stitch has a context uniquely yours."

The band is captured on camera again during a heated performance in July 2007 at LA's House Of Blues. SIPA PRESS/REX FEATURES

James strikes a pose during the outdoor CBS *Early Show* concert series, held in New York on September 5, 2007.

The paparazzi snatch a shot of Adam cruising on his motorbike near his home in LA, on a hot summer's day in 2009.

The boys pose for casual pictures outside a New York TV studio in September 2010, shortly after an appearance on the *Late Show* with David Letterman. EVERETT COLLECTION/REX FEATURES

Adam celebrates the reunion of vintage rock group The Beach Boys with a rendition of their track 'Surfer Girl' at the 2012 Grammy Awards in LA. Here, he is pictured with members Mike Love and David Marks. PICTUREGROUP/REX FEATURES

The boys make their grand entrance to the 2012 Grammy Awards at LA's Staples Center, with Adam in particular looking quite at home among musical royalty. DAN MACMEDAN/WIREIMAGE

Mickey is captured live in action in 2012 at the Grammy Nominations Concert at Bridgestone Arena, Nashville, Tennessee.
FREDERICK BREEDON IV/FILMMAGIC

Matt is pictured at the same concert, which saw nominations announced live on primetime TV. Millions would go on to watch the official ceremony. FREDERICK BREEDON IV/FILMMAGIC

Jesse too is photographed at the Grammy Nominations Concert.
FREDERICK BREEDON IV/FILMMAGIC

Adam shows off the tattooed forearms that would famously see grown women swoon during episodes of *The Voice* as he performs with James at the Grammy Nominations Concert.
KEVIN WINTER/WIREIMAGE

Adam poses with his *The Voice* co-stars Blake Shelton, Christina Aguilera and Cee Lo Green at a 2011 NBC press conference to promote the show. BROADIMAGE/REX FEATURES

James and PJ attend KIIS FM's 2012 Jingle Ball, held at the Nokia Theatre LA Live. TOMMASO BODDI/WIREIMAGE

Adam performs a rendition of 'Stereohearts' with his musical partner Travie McCoy of Gym Class Heroes at 102.7 KIIS FM's Wango Tango 2012 in Carson, California. GREGG DEGUIRE/FILMMAGIC

The boys indulge in a publicity shoot in Paris, capturing on film the essence of Maroon 5. SIPA PRESS/REX FEATURES

Adam cultivated a moody atmosphere with a combination of jet black wallpaper and heavy burgundy velvet curtains, shielding the night owl from the morning sun. Then he plastered the walls with photography by Mark Seliger and artwork by Shepard Fairey; silkscreened Andy Warhol paintings blended with the occasional contemporary work such as a black and white portrait of Kurt Cobain or Bob Dylan.

That this was a bachelor pad was without question – with dark theatrical tones at every turn, there was nothing gender-neutral here. Thanks to the décor, Adam's obsession with music was equally unmistakeable: there was a petite Wurlitzer grand piano, an imitation jukebox, his trusty guitar and a huge collection of vintage records strewn across the floor. Outside of the studio, music was still his life.

A few macabre touches referenced the noir side of his tastes: a metal skull by the bedside, a lamp shaped like an AK47 and a painting of a machine gun taking prominent place in the centre of one wall. While the bedroom was intentionally dark and moody, full-length windows covered the entire living room wall.

Finally, in contrast to the interior, the terrace was pure white. With its Moorish architectural touches, it looked more Moroccan than American; the palm-tree fringed gardens it looked out upon gave a bird's-eye view of the city. And of course, a house would not be a home without a man's best friend: Adam's golden retriever, Frankie, had his paw prints etched into the concrete around the entrance.

No sooner had Adam decorated his dream home than it was time to start work on album number two. "Our album is going to be much more out there if I have anything to do with it," Jesse had playfully threatened. "I want our next record to sound like Stevie Wonder meets Radiohead meets Steely Dan meets the Red Hot Chili Peppers meets D'Angelo meets Frank Zappa."

It was an ambitious list of influences, but they intended to incorporate as many as possible. The location for their studio sessions was a 10-bedroom mansion in Laurel Canyon, originally home to escapologist Harry Houdini. The ancient house had history, with Mick Jagger, Jimi Hendrix, David Bowie and even the Beatles also having formerly stayed there.

However, it may also have been home to some unwelcome and perhaps malevolent visitors. According to rumour, the house had been haunted since 1918, when a man had pushed his lover to her death over the balcony. Spectral presences had been detected there ever since.

When Red Hot Chili Peppers recorded their platinum-selling album *Blood Sugar Sex Magik* on the premises, their terrified drummer, Chad Smith, refused to live on-site, renting out a home nearby instead. Guitarist John Frusciante, on the other hand, claimed that the ghosts were friendly, even opting to masturbate in front of one. In honour of their time at the mansion, the group even published a group photo complete with an un-explained orb, which they believed to be a spiritual presence, on their album cover.

Slipknot singer Corey Taylor had also captured mysterious orbs on camera, which he claimed hovered near the thermostat in his room, inter-mittently changing the temperature. As a mask-wearing heavy metal group proudly described as 'satanic' by some of their followers, they didn't seem the type to be fearful of ghosts – and yet drummer Joey Jordison had been equally uneasy, claiming a cold presence had walked right through him in the basement. The experience had prompted him to avoid the room altogether for the rest of his stay.

Something about this mansion had the effect of inspiring formerly sensible musicians – the type that would usually scornfully dismiss the idea of spirits inhabiting a home – with terror. Inexplicable footsteps would patrol corridors, doors would swing open and closed for no apparent reason, and malevolent figures would haunt residents' dreams.

However, Maroon 5 did not report any ghostly presences – to them, the mansion was more notable for its role in recording Stevie Wonder's *Songs In The Key Of Life*. The quintet would descend on the mansion daily, with Jesse and James making it their home. In a bid to continue their relation-ship with Ryan and hold on to some of the history that had shaped the band, they elected him as the album's creative director. He would have a significant say in how the songs were written, while old friend Jason Cader – who had engineered the demos for 'Harder To Breathe' and 'This Love' – made up the final member of their seven-piece party.

As they started to compose tracks, while there was a fortunate lack of tension between Matt and Ryan, it quickly emerged that the band would need to adapt to the former's style. "I would be lying if I said it wasn't difficult for us," Adam would later confess. "When you change a member, it takes some adjusting. We were all under pressure to make this big, amazing second record and on top we had to adjust to this new situation . . . [Matt] is a straight-ahead rock drummer, whereas Ryan was a bit jazzier."

Yet this new rockier feel would be appreciated when it came to dark subject matter such as 'Wake Up Call' – a revenge-fuelled murder fantasy told from the perspective of a man whose girlfriend has sexually betrayed him. After finding a six-foot love rival in bed with her, he responds by killing them both. Hypocritically, he's no stranger to cheating himself, as he admits when he adds furiously that his lover had played him at his "own game". Asking tentatively if he's done the wrong thing, it sounds as though he may be edging towards remorse; he quickly erases that impression when he laments immediately afterwards that his victim's heart is still beating – in his eyes, the only mistake he's made lies in failing to finish the job properly.

The frenetic new percussion style introduced by Matt would fit the tone of the song, with drum strokes sonically doubling as gunshots. As Adam was keen to point out, the character depicted was fictional, bearing no resemblance to emotions he might have felt in real life. Rather, he'd been motivated to write the track in a bid to escape from the stereotypes that hounded the group ever since its release of shamelessly tender ballads like 'She Will Be Loved'. In the aftermath, they were compared less frequently to the soul idols that took pride of place on his iPod playlist and more often to less respected teen icons such as Ronan Keating and the Backstreet Boys.

Adam wanted to transform himself from the weak, insipid, hopeless romantic that cynics saw him as – the kind who waited around for women in the pouring rain – into someone darker, edgier and more aggressive. In doing so, he'd almost written a miniature film noir script for himself. But he wanted to live a little more dangerously and to take chances with his artistic output, enthusing, "It would be cool to have something so dark as a radio hit."

And it certainly was a chart hit that he had in mind when he devised it – to measure its appeal, he'd played the early version to his much younger brother and sister to get their verdicts. "If you can get a kid singing the words to a song after they heard it for the first time, it's a hit. Kids have no censor. [If they don't like something]. They'll say, 'This is shitty!'" Adam commented, before adding jokingly, "Well, hopefully they're not foul-mouthed little bastards!"

More light-hearted were the throbbing, rhythmic beats of pure pop track 'If I Never See Your Face Again'. There were the same traces of furious sexual jealousy, with Adam telling a summer fling that he burns to find out if she's with another man, but it stops short of obsession – it's still casual enough that, if he never sees her face again, he won't mind.

'Kiwi', a mischievous track which talks about a sweet kiwi fruit that leaves juices dripping down Adam's chin, is an obvious euphemism for oral sex. In case the message didn't transmit – and he would later joke about some of the racier lyrics "going over grandparents' heads" – there was a more explicit line about a woman spreading her legs across the bed until he makes her "shake". After chipping away at the preconceptions of Maroon 5 as a play-it-safe boy band, another way for Adam to break boundaries was to introduce an increasingly sexual element to his work. 'Kiwi' was the lyrical sequel in this sense to the liberated vibe of 'This Love'.

'Goodnight Goodnight' is the twin brother of 'Wake Up Call' – except that, in the former, Adam's character is not contemplating doing away with a love rival but speaking instead of killing himself. A fight with a woman leaves him facing a bleak, hopeless future without her and, consumed by defeat, he bids the world goodnight.

'Better That We Break' captures all of his former emotions at losing Jane, but with a few more recent images added to it: for example, when he sings that the city looks nice from his vantage point, he is referring to his new home in the Hollywood Hills. Yet all the fruits of the material wealth he's accumulated fade into insignificance against the loss of his lover. He can't live with or without their traumatic relationship, and eventually the turmoil leads him to break it off once and for all.

Similarly, 'Nothing Lasts Forever' deals with the sad realisation that a relationship has run its course. Adam's lover is with him in body but not in spirit, and while make-up sex provides a tempting yet ineffectual sticking plaster to hide the wound, it cannot heal the gulf between them. He talks of the protective wall he's built around his heart and how he secretly hopes it will fall down when he's caught off guard, but, in the cold light of day, both parties have their drawbridges up.

The final two songs of the sessions – 'Won't Go Home Without You' and 'I'm Not Falling Apart' – followed the same tragic-romantic theme. With subject matter including murder, suicide and break-ups, all fuelled by passionate relationships turned sour, it might have seemed that all of the album's subject matter was dark – and yet Adam was making no apologies.

"Honestly, the saddest moments of my life are the ones I write about," he shrugged. "I can only really write when I'm feeling down, which is a powerful thing, to feel that way, so you have to capitalise on it. It's almost as if, 'Wow, I feel shit, I'd better make use of this, otherwise it'll be a complete waste!'"

He added, "I think you are put on this Earth to do what is natural and what is natural for me is using the lyrics that I write or the music that I write with my band as therapy."

Of the 30 songs which the band demoed, these eight tracks were the strongest. Now they needed the production team to record them: Mark 'Spike' Stent and Mike Elizondo – the latter of whom had famously played double bass live onstage with Guns N' Roses when, at the 1992 VMAs, they'd performed the single 'November Rain'.

Together with the production duo, Maroon 5 started the recording process at Conway Studios. This location had history for the band – they'd made the demo that got them signed to Octone there, as well as various Kara's Flowers demos prior to that – and it had also been the location where, as a teenager, Adam had been entertained by his first stripper.

Here they played songs by the Police, Prince, Michael Jackson and Talking Heads on repeat to inspire a vibe for the backing tracks. (For example, Jackson's 'Off The Wall' would provide the inspiration for 'If I Never See Your Face Again'.) After this phase, the meticulous group booked into a third LA studio, Glenwood Place in Burbank, to "listen ad nauseam" to their work thus far.

"Eventually realising that there were a few musical loose ends to be tied up, we went in for two additional sessions, with Eric Valentine and Mark Endert respectively, for fresh perspectives and fresh ears," Mickey would recall.

These sessions yielded 'Can't Stop', a tale of an obsessive yet unrequited passion for a former flame who continually inhabits Adam's thoughts, yet never calls. The track borrowed classic Kara's Flowers phrases, speaking of a woman "tattooed" on his mind. 'A Little Of Your Time' also emerged, where Adam begs for a chance to heal a relationship with his words, while 'Back At Your Door' continues the theme of going round in circles because he cannot bear to disentangle himself from a romance.

Then there was 'Make You Wonder', the final track and the one that would form the first part of Maroon 5's comeback. Aside from an October 2006 appearance at a launch night for Justin Timberlake's William Rast clothing line – which saw Adam and Justin harmonising onstage together on 'This Love' to celebrate the occasion – Maroon 5 had been out of the public eye for months. Their comeback had to be a momentous one, as the audience's response would dictate whether or not the band was heading for the dreaded – yet frequently inevitable – sophomore slump.

Despite the overwhelming pressure, there was one vital difference between this album and its predecessor – the band members were now adamant that, instead of calculating crowd-pleasers, they would only release tracks that expressed who they were as individuals. Idolising and emulating other artists had been a large part of growing up – after all, it had inspired the group to start playing in the first place – but now they'd moved on and found confidence in what they could offer as themselves.

"There's only one Bruce Springsteen, there's only one John Lennon, there's only one David Bowie, there's only one Kurt Cobain," Adam reasoned. "Every day goes by and I say, 'Why can't I be one of those?' I finally realised, after many years, that I don't *want* to be one of those people. The more you act like something you're not, the less genuine you are – so I want to embrace who *I* am and what *I've* become."

In his view, the way to make musical history was not to try to be the next Lennon but to become a figure in his own right, one that future generations might be desperate to emulate. Achieving the coveted yet elusive status of a legend came not from copying another person's career, but from making one's own unique.

That was the ideal the band had in mind when, on April 1, 2007, they released 'Make Me Wonder'. At first listen, it might have sounded like the archetypal Maroon 5 loss-of-love story, but it was also symbolic of the group's stance on something deeper: the thorny issues of US politics.

Penned during a final songwriting session, it was born from an existing skeletal lyric about losing Jane, which had been written several years previously but never released. The band had unearthed the old track purely by coincidence, but it then occurred to Adam that his political anger could be inserted into a relationship song, that the emotions each elicited were almost interchangeable.

While relationships typically ended as a result of deceit or betrayal, Adam felt similar pain when he perceived that an unscrupulous government had torn his much-loved homeland apart, just as a cheated lover might argue that their dishonest partner had destroyed the relationship. The most controversial issue for him was the Iraq War, started due to George Bush's suspicions that the Middle Eastern nation was harbouring weapons of mass destruction. This was later revealed to be untrue, meaning that thousands had lost their lives needlessly; Adam shared the feeling of many Americans that the President had known his claims had little foundation all along.

Incorporating this fury into his song lyrics placed him in the same category as Rage Against The Machine and System Of A Down. The latter had once declared that presidents should be responsible for fighting the wars they waged, rather than risking the lives of ordinary people – the same conclusion reached by both Adam and Jesse, after some fierce debate.

While the political references in 'Make Me Wonder' were cloaked in the erotic memory of being lost between someone's thighs, it suited Adam. "It's one of the most difficult things in the world to make a political song without coming off as a total arse and preachy," he later agonised to MTV, "all the things that I hate about a lot of songwriting. So I didn't want to overtly say it. I just wanted to allude to it."

What resulted was "a bizarre hybrid of me being in a failing relationship at the time combined with a new element of my failure to understand or trust what's going on with the leadership of our country."

Yet it almost never made it to radio at all, as Adam was far from convinced that an ancient demo could be album material. In fact, he openly disliked the track – but the label thought differently, urging the band back into the studio to create a new chorus that would complete the song.

"The initial demo that Adam made was minus the 'Gimme something to believe in' part and we knew that something felt incomplete," Jesse later recalled, "so we would spend time trying to force writing a part, which never really yields anything good."

The solution would finally come during a session of hard partying in Las Vegas, where the distractions of Sin City removed the pressure from the writing process. What had previously felt as torturous as pulling teeth was now child's play and, within days, they'd perfected the chorus at the studio at the legendary Palms Hotel.

While the band remained a little sceptical, trusted producer Mark Endert fused their myriad emotions together in a reinvented track that was suitably drum-and-bass heavy. Their collaboration transformed the track from a rock'n'roll style to a seventies funk vibe.

"I decided to make the drums and bass the loudest thing in the track and keep the vocals tucked, kind of like on a Prince record," Endert elaborated. "Two of the tracks I had been listening to as a reference were 'Billie Jean' by Michael Jackson and 'Kiss' by Prince. I remembered them as drum-heavy, but I was shocked by how loud the drums actually were on those cuts. I decided I wanted to go in the same direction, to keep the listener's head going up and down."

As well as turning up the drums, he sought to combine genres to give the track a modern Maroon 5 feel, and also to blend electronic programming with live playing – an unusual mix, but one for which the group was renowned.

"The idea was to make it contemporary and urban and also to make it classic seventies and early eighties sounding like their first album," Mark added. "I was referencing many records from the seventies and eighties before working on this track and the pulse that makes your head go up and down has the disco-like feel that's typical for that era."

The newly invigorated track met with the band's approval, ending the disdain they'd felt for it for years. Yet ironically for a song that had been added to the album as a mere afterthought, its popularity was explosive – and it would net Maroon 5 its first US number one.

Even prior to its release, it hit the top spot on iTunes thanks to a video that transformed the humdrum Los Angeles International Airport building into a "surreal and sexually charged fantasy airport", as Adam described it. The month after its release, the track launched itself from number 64 straight to number one – the biggest jump in the history of the *Billboard* chart.

This time around, there was something edgier about the group – and their ever-increasing popularity would be accentuated still further with the release of the album, entitled *It Won't Be Soon Before Long*. The seemingly nonsensical title was developed early in the recording process to remind the group to be patient. In other words, before long, 'soon' will become the present day.

"It's kind of a more eloquent version of 'Hurry up and wait'," Adam explained to a bemused MTV interviewer. "Ringo Starr had these Ringo-isms in the Beatles where he would say something that didn't make sense, but if you thought about it in more abstract terms, it makes perfect sense. It's one of those. I think it fits everything that happened in our career. It helped us become more patient – and it's easy to get ahead of yourself in a band. I get an idea and I want it to happen straight away."

When the album was released on May 22, 2007, it instantly made it to number one on iTunes, boasting more than 50,000 presales. While this lifted Maroon 5 to a whole new level of notoriety, it also meant the band would soon become a target for media mockery. The experience should have been one of elation, but overall it would heighten their exposure to the dark side of fame.

Not only were they the victims of internet trolls, but, to Adam's embarrassment, he had to fend off rumours that he'd outed Russian tennis champion Maria Sharapova as a bad lover. At six feet two inches tall, the muscular sportswoman wasn't classically feminine, but thanks to her long blonde hair, blue eyes and baby face, she had become quite an international sex symbol – and there was enormous prurient interest in her life between the sheets.

Adam had been invited to perform at her 18th birthday party two years previously and had barely seen her since. However, mischievous showbiz reporters didn't let the facts get in the way of a good story and began to report on a torrid love affair.

Before he could deny it, a Russian English-language magazine, *Exile*, took the speculation a step further by publishing a piece of sexual satire. "She wouldn't make any noise during sex," Adam was quoted as saying. "I can't tell you how disappointed I was. I really thought, like a lot of guys, that she'd be the loud, screaming type, but instead she just lay there like a dead frog. She even got angry if I started to moan, saying it ruined her concentration. It was so disillusionary that I went on Paxil for a month afterwards. Really, it was much more of a shock than when I found out there's no such thing as the Easter Bunny!"

The piece was clearly satirical, poking fun at Sharapova's infamous 110-decibel screams on the court – the same frequency as a lion's roar and so loud that they were said to break the sound barrier. Many speculated that it was not an involuntary sound driven by the exertion of the sport, but a calculated bid to destroy her opponent's concentration. Her reputation as one of the loudest players in the game, combined with sexual innuendo, made for a good gag as far as *Exile*'s editors were concerned – but Adam was incensed. He contacted the magazine, asking for a retraction and threatening to sue, but its cool and collected publisher, American expat Mark Ames, countered that it was "throwaway satire", written in five minutes in a California hotel room, adding, "Americans are the most gullible fucking morons on Planet Earth."

Yet, unfortunately for Adam, numerous US media sources picked up the story and republished it as fact. Faced with the bogus quotes that formed news snippets in almost every major gossip magazine – often edited down in a way that made the story seem more plausible – he was furious about the impact it might have on his reputation.

Days after assuring the nation that he wasn't the type to kiss and tell, Adam faced new allegations that he'd been captured on a sex tape. This story couldn't instantly be dismissed as mischief either – despite his earlier comments against sex tapes, he had appeared naked in the 'This Love' video. Surely then, doing the deed was, for a sexually liberated attention addict like him, just a small step further?

Some papers had speculated that sex tapes may have been a lucrative career move for the likes of Kim Kardashian (*if* she had personally allowed her particular tape to be released), but Adam didn't need the boost; though of course, in a society of double standards, their release didn't carry the same negative connotation for men.

He was quick to adamantly refute this story too. "You don't make a sex tape if you're a celebrity," he declared. "The only reason why you would make a sex tape is if you secretly wanted it to get out. Listen, if I wanted to have a sex tape out there, I'd have 10 – but it's just in poor taste to divulge the gory details of your sex life in public. It's just really not attractive to me. It's not that I'm a square or anything – there are just some things you need to keep sacred and private."

Struggling under the weight of all the fake stories, Adam decided to play the media at their own game, making a cheeky statement controversial enough to detract attention from the rumours. "Every male secretly wants to have sex with Brad Pitt," he would casually tell gay lifestyle magazine *Out*, "but that's a given."

Yet beneath the surface, behind the jokey bravado, he was often deeply wounded by the media's perception of him. While it was evidently nothing personal – his celebrity status had simply entangled him in a ruthless international quest to deliver the biggest headlines – he struggled with the sense of injustice that came from feeling misunderstood.

"When you are successful on this level, people tend to want to break you down," he commented knowingly. "I don't think I will be completely fulfilled until I win everybody's love and adoration because, maybe I'm just completely crazy, but I always feel like people misunderstand us for whatever reason – and I want people to get it straight, so that's what keeps me going. I'm not asking that everybody likes us because that's impossible, but I am asking that everybody understands where we're coming from."

That ambition would prove a woefully lost cause as, by July, yet more controversy was in store. 'Wake Up Call' had been chosen as the next single and the video would feature Adam in the role of a villain. Armed with a loaded gun, he would proceed to act out the lyrics of the song, catching his girlfriend in bed with a secret lover and shooting him dead in revenge.

While the song had originally been intended to convey a double murder, the video would reveal Adam's girlfriend helping him to conceal the death of the other man, before delivering the monumental understatement: "We both fucked up." Adam is ultimately discovered and pays for his crime by being executed in the electric chair.

Fearing that more conservative parents would boycott their stations, the major music channels opted for damage limitation, changing the words "We both fucked up" to the less inflammatory "We both screwed up," and replacing Adam's execution with a shot of him sleeping in a prison cell. The sex scenes were also toned down to make them more family-friendly.

Yet while the twisted revenge fantasy was purely fictional and, even pre-edit, contained nothing worse than the contents of an average crime novel, it sparked a public outcry. The video would eventually be viewed online more than 14 million times and, amazingly, thousands of those viewers would interpret it as sexist.

Complaining of artistic double standards, Adam hit back: "That's just really ridiculous because if a girl was writing these songs, they wouldn't be sexist – they would be empowering. That's completely insane. The video is definitely controversial and I understand that, but you have to understand at the same time it's a video. It's obviously fictional . . . I'm not a violent person, I'm simply telling a story and if you can't differentiate between what is real and what is fiction then you don't deserve my attention anyway, so I don't really give a shit . . . it's just fake, it's pretend and entertainment exists. If I was a woman in a video where I was killing a man, everybody would be cheering. Also my character gets the chair. He's not exactly winning. He's obviously a prick."

As furious as Adam was at the accusation – in his eyes yet another example of how he was stereotyped and misunderstood – part of him relished the chance to step outside of the safety zone. The controversy merely distinguished him from the generic, flavourless boy bands of the music world.

"It's better to offend people than to fit in perfectly," he continued. "Making that video was a direct reaction to how we were treated in the culture which was, 'Oh look, this safe band and bring your kids because they never say the F-word and they're so sweet and look how cute they are' and all that . . . we don't want to be the safe go-to Mickey Mouse band that they portrayed us as for the first album, so we wanted to mix it up a little bit [and] I'm glad we offended people."

Tellingly, following the single's release on August 7, sales remained strong, indicating that the backlash hadn't lost them their fanbase. The band's tour also rewarded them with plenty of sell-out shows, as they travelled the world with an unconventional mission: to stay totally carbon-neutral on the road. Their sponsors – climate change organisation Global Cool – were working with them to reduce the amount of carbon emissions produced.

It seemed a hopeless aspiration to fly and drive their way through the USA and beyond without leaving a 'carbon footprint' – particularly when they travelled further in a few months than the average holidaymaker might in an entire decade. But still, the band was donating $1 from each concert ticket to buy offsetting vouchers. As Adam warned: "Our world is in a serious predicament right now and we all need to play a role in reversing the catastrophic effects of global warming."

Another cause on his mind was the war against homophobia. To raise awareness, he took part in a comedy sketch on *Saturday Night Live* which aired on September 29, ridiculing the fundamentalist views of Iranian President Mahmoud Ahmadinejad. The President had attended New York's Columbia University for a debate the previous week and left students open-mouthed when, after casually claiming that the Holocaust was a myth, he announced: "In Iran, we don't have homosexuals like in your country . . . we do not have this phenomenon."

Of course, what he'd meant was that practising homosexual acts was forbidden and punishable by death, rendering open gay couples in the country non-existent. Yet his outright denial invited mockery, with comedian Andy Samberg obliging on the improvised R&B love song 'I Ran'.

Posing as Mahmoud's lover, he crooned: "You can deny the Holocaust all you want, but you can't deny that there's something between us," adding, "I know you say there are no gays in Iran, but you're in New York now, baby!"

Adam joined in the chorus, while *Brokeback Mountain* actor Jake Gyllenhaal – portrayed as the gay love interest in the song – made a last-minute cameo at the end, flashing peace signs at the audience.

A minority of viewers regarded the gag as in bad taste, feeling it trivialised the serious issue of homophobic prejudice for entertainment. In their eyes, it also made light of hard-line Muslim fundamentalists who viewed gay lifestyles as a culturally transmitted disease and whose protests could one day threaten Western liberties. Yet again, Adam had found himself at the centre of another controversy, but over the ensuing years he would prove his commitment to gay rights was sincere.

★ ★ ★

Meanwhile, Maroon 5's latest tour started to progress. Highlights included a sell-out show at New York's Madison Square Garden. That night onstage, Adam broke into 'Nothing Lasts Forever', which borrowed its chorus from 'Heard 'Em Say', before announcing a very special guest to join him on the latter: Kanye West. A white soul singer and black rapper sharing the same stage was still an unusual sight as, for the most part, singers of different ethnicities were still racially segregated due to the unbalanced perception that they belonged to different genres and commanded different audiences.

The following month, on November 19, 2007, the group released the new album's third single, 'Won't Go Home Without You'. The video depicted a turbulent love affair, with Adam storming out on a woman and then repentantly roaming the city streets in a bid to find her. When he finally does, he is too late to make amends and she is already with another man. Multi-instrumentalist Jesse is seen playing both piano and guitar.

While the single failed to reach the Top 40 in the US or UK, it included a much-praised version of John Lennon's peace anthem 'Happy Christmas (War Is Over)' as a B-side. However, the album had surpassed all expectations, prompting the label to plan a re-release. In between concerts, Maroon 5 worked to perfect some bonus tracks for the CD: 'Infatuation' and 'Until You're Over Me' dealt with a struggle to let go of a love affair, while 'Miss You Love You' saw a slightly sadistic Adam dole out some of the pain he had experienced himself by refusing to accept his ex's increasingly desperate affections. On the aptly titled 'Losing My Mind', his lyric took the concept of obsessive love to a whole new level, via stalking a woman by parking his car outside her home. His anger that his love was unrequited led to a promise that he'd make it impossible for her to let go. 'Story' – a B-side that had featured on 'Wake Up Call' – was also added to the track-list for the rerelease.

The final bonus track was a remake of 'If I Never See Your Face Again' – complete with duel partner Rihanna, who didn't need much persuading to take part. "I was like, 'Any song – I don't care if it's a song I don't like – I want to do it because Maroon 5 is dope!' " she excitedly told GMTV. Her infatuation was reciprocated, with Adam mesmerised by her "unbelievable talent". "We were just in the studio messing around with her," he would recall, "and I was listening to her sing in a vocal booth without any effects. She's the real deal. She's badass!"

The collaboration had been a welcome challenge for both parties.

Rihanna's voice on the track was deep and velvety, while Adam's was delivered in a much higher falsetto, providing an unusual contrast. What was more, the genre was new to Rihanna; coming from an R&B/reggae background, the closest she'd ever come to rocky pop was on her single 'Shut Up And Drive'. Eager to experiment with new styles and contexts, both parties were full of excited anticipation.

The video shoot itself, however, would be quite literally like watching paint dry. A series of different sets had been created for the recording, which required repainting between takes. It meant a lot of waiting around, with only a chemical scent for company. Adam and Rihanna hit it off though; driven by his passion for fashion, he even volunteered to assist with her styling to alleviate the boredom.

Ahead of the album, the single was released on May 15, 2008, to a flurry of reviews. However, a small number of journalists who'd had a sneak preview behind the scenes at the shoot had inaccurately branded the video "high end erotica", ultimately leading to an anticlimax when reviewers realised there was nothing more than playful flirtation at work. Thus *Digital Spy*'s criticism: "The sexual chemistry radar of the pairing registers at zero" – but Adam begged to differ.

"I always find it hard to concentrate," he quipped in reference to his ADHD, "and she doesn't make it any easier!"

Meanwhile, Rihanna, who in previous months had stated she was almost exclusively attracted to black men, seemed willing to make an exception for Adam – one of the rare white men she deemed 'hot'.

"I don't do a lot of videos where I have so much chemistry with the other artist," she explained. "It's really intense."

Both Rihanna and Maroon 5 would be releasing their albums in the summer, so the track would appear on Rihanna's *Good Girl Gone Bad: Reloaded* on June 2, while the reissue of *It Won't Be Soon Before Long* was scheduled for July 8. In both the UK and Australia, where the CD was released a week early, an additional bonus track was included – a remix of 'Wake Up Call' by Mark Ronson, featuring vocals from Mary J. Blige. All around the world, a bonus DVD also came as part of the package, with four official music videos and a live concert recorded in Montreal the previous year.

The band remained proud of 'If I See Your Face Again', their sonic ambassador for the reissue – not least because the track had aided charity too. Jesse's father had taken a series of photographs for the album version of the song, compiling a video which the band donated to Amnesty International. The charity's mission was to promote human rights universally irrespective of gender, race, religion, ethnicity or sexual preference, and its activism had helped to release tens of thousands political prisoners over the years – including Burmese opposition leader Aung San Suu Kyi, a female politician whose National League for Democracy had won the popular vote in Burma, but who had been oppressed by the military and kept under house arrest. Amnesty's campaign against the death penalty had also led to its abolition in two thirds of the world's countries, in comparison to just 16 which refrained from capital punishment at the time they'd started raising awareness.

Adam continued the political theme when he joined forces with fellow Octone Records singer K'naan, a Somalian rapper with a sound described by the artists as fusing "Bob Marley, American hip-hop and protest poetry", on the track 'Bang Bang'. K'naan, who had emigrated to the US as a child, was raised in a culture that the Western world typically associated with corruption, piracy and brutal tribal violence.

What was different about K'naan was that, while the likes of Akon falsely bragged about doing time in jail to become a status symbol, he avoided the typical gangsta rap clichés. While many privileged Americans played upon the supposed glamour of guns and power, he'd seen that lifestyle and its corrosive, corrupting nature at first hand.

"All Somalis know that gangsterism isn't to brag about," he declared. "The kids that I was growing up with would wear baggy tracksuit pants and a little jacket from Zellers or something and they'd walk into school and all the cool kids would be like, 'Ah man, look at those Somalis. Yo, you're a punk!' And the other kid won't say nothing, but that kid, probably, has killed 15 people."

While many of those who glamorised the gun culture had rarely seen violence outside of computer games and rap-video simulations, for K'naan it was too raw, real and close to home to trivialise. Even in Rexdale, where he grew up, Somalian culture often prevailed and he lost some of those in his social group to suicide, murder and prison sentences. K'naan's focus was on staying alive – and making music that conveyed his wrought emotions.

Although he wasn't a household name, by the time Adam joined him on a track, he'd already collaborated with Will.i.am, the Roots, Mos Def and Damian Marley. On 'Bang Bang', he and Adam would turn the gun metaphor around to represent not hate but love, telling of a woman who shoots a man in the heart with love in her eye. The duo asked what love was without pain alongside it and what pain was if not the inspiration to write songs – something which matched Adam's own sentiments exactly.

The two main subjects that he wrote about were now love and politics – and he soon returned to the latter theme. The backdrop was a world tour that would see Maroon 5 visit every continent with the exception of Antarctica. While they were on the road, there was another US presidential election – following fresh terrorism threats from Muslims who objected to Christians' refusal to accept Allah as the only god.

A frustrated Jesse spoke scornfully: "It seems hard to imagine that any divine force out there (an all-powerful, all-knowing entity that we could call God, or Allah, or Krishna, or Boran, or Shango, or Thixo, Gaunab or Tsui, or any other name that humans have given the unfathomable) would actually want to kill people who used a different name for IT! I like to think of the different interpretations of this divine force as cultural nicknames. They're endearing: sometimes people have lots of nicknames. It's not surprising that God would have lots too. God is very popular!

"No single person on this planet actually knows what God's will is for humans," he added, "but most people agree that God is interested in us leading basic moral lives – don't kill others, try not to cause suffering, etc. The golden rule sounds pretty good to me – or, as the classic movie *Bill And Ted's Excellent Adventures* so eloquently put it, 'Be excellent to each other and party on, dudes!'"

Jesse's live-and-let-live policy seemed entirely logical and reasoned. By November, however, as the album's final single, 'Goodnight Goodnight' – a Brazil and UK only release featuring a video with a cameo from Ryan – hit the music channels, something the band regarded as a step toward social justice was dramatically overturned.

Just six months earlier, in a ground-breaking victory for homosexuals, the California Supreme Court had ruled that gay couples were allowed to legally marry. Yet thanks to a ballot proposition to overturn the motion, the state elections in November invalidated all of that. A new provision was added to the California constitution ruling that "only marriage between a man and a woman is valid or recognised" and the very progress that gay people had been celebrating was snatched away from them.

The ballot had been close, with just 56 per cent of voters supporting the ban on equal rights to marriage. For Jesse, it was the party with the most financial power, rather than the best policies, that had won on the day – another indictment of an inequality-based capitalist society.

"People who want to deny equal rights to homosexuals," he noted, "spent the second most amount of money on any election category other than the presidency."

In response to the ruling, Adam took part in an interview with gay magazine *Pride Source*, asking incredulously, "In saying certain people aren't allowed to marry, what leg do you have to stand on there? Unless you can admit that you're putting yourself above them, then there's no argument. Otherwise you would say, 'Everyone has the right to marry.'"

For Adam, the very concept of marriage – straight or gay – was a fascinating yet terrifying prospect. While he was romantic enough to idealise the thought of committing to spending his life with someone, he was fazed by the fact that, in the West, more marriages failed than succeeded. If he didn't get married, he reasoned, then he'd never have to go through the trauma of a divorce. On the other hand, it was better to have loved and lost than not to have loved at all – and he remained undecided.

Yet what irked him most was that there was no evidence that gay marriages were any more likely to crumble than those of their straight peers – so why should they be denied the chance to try?

"Look at the divorce rate and all the things that go wrong with marriage," Adam urged. "Whether it's gay or straight, there are issues with it. Clearly people have a hard time staying together and that's just a sad truth about marriage in our society. People should be allowed to succeed and fail at marriage as they so desire.

"I was brought up to believe that everybody is on a level playing field," he added. "I judge people based on their character. If you have a friend who decides to do certain things in their own private time – even if they're straight – whatever the fuck they're into, that's fine. It just simply doesn't affect the way I feel about a person."

Some disapproved on religious grounds, claiming that God had declared marriage as between a man and a woman. According to the Bible, those who loved the same sex would not be granted entry to Heaven. But the religious theory still didn't account for why a God-fearing community needed to go beyond believing homosexuality was wrong by imposing their rules and beliefs on others.

"It's not our business," Adam would insist. "I don't know why we're obsessed with making everything in this country our business all the time. Someone's sexual preference is their sexual preference. Let's move on."

It wouldn't be the last the world from Adam about the need for homo-sexual equality, but his parting shot for now was unambiguous: if he was ever voted in as President, legalising gay marriage would be the first thing he'd do.

8

Stepping Back Into The Shadows

THEY'd had a number one album in 2008, and yet ironically, a matter of months later, the members of Maroon 5 were reduced to living in a garage – all for the love of music, of course.

Adam's house had been undergoing renovations and, instead of succumbing to the temptations of notoriously decadent hotel the Chateau Marmont – former home to the likes of James Dean and Jim Morrison – he'd decided to rent out a new home.

Following previous tours, Adam had been a regular resident at the Marmont – a sprawling yet secluded fairytale castle set high in the hills above the Sunset Strip, making it the perfect location to escape from city life. A stay here seemed almost obligatory for any self-respecting musician or creative artist passing through; yet the hotel also came with an unwritten guarantee – for better or for worse – of debauchery.

According to one hotel review website, it was responsible for "more celebrity excess and self-destruction than Caligula's boudoir", and this wasn't mere artistic embellishment – the hotel's colourful history spoke for itself.

Courtney Love had once emerged slurring from her suite, high on a cocktail of heroin, alcohol and antidepressants, to take part in an interview stark naked. Morrison had almost died on-site due to a drunken fall from the roof. Dean had leapt from a window by way of introduction when auditioning for the lead role in the legendary film *Rebel Without A Cause*. Unsurprisingly, given his flamboyance, he got the part.

Red Hot Chili Peppers created their chart-topping track 'By The Way' at the hotel too, but guitarist John Frusciante – a self-confessed heroin addict who, at that time, had needle track marks all over his arms – was described at the time by an interviewer as a miserable "skeleton with thin skin" and was banned from residence altogether by the following day.

In contrast, while Adam had whiled away much of his time off at the hotel in previous years, he'd indulged in nothing more serious than a few puffs of marijuana and a penchant for calorie-laden burgers. But, with those in the know claiming the atmosphere induced debauchery, he knew that next time he might not be so lucky. Creative flames were both ignited and extinguished in equal measure here, with musicians often having brief flashes of artistic brilliance before descending into addiction-related hell. Determined not to fall prey to Chateau Marmont's many distractions, Adam found his temporary home and, with the help of the band, converted its garage into an impromptu rehearsal studio.

As sound engineer Noah Passovoy, who worked on their demos, observed: "They just kind of threw up four walls and soundproofed it so that anyone could be making noise in there at all hours and not annoying the neighbours! The biggest problem was the ceilings because we couldn't build past the beams of the garage, so you had maybe seven foot ceilings! It was just kind of a box."

The challenge was "to cram, physically, as many things as possible into the room" – and with a drum kit, guitar and bass amps, keyboards, a vocal booth and a designated Pro Tools production rig all swallowing space in a dark, dingy garage, that was no easy feat. It was even a challenge to receive an internet signal in a box almost resembling an underground cavern – but the band thrived on the feeling of being cut off from the outside world.

One spring evening, they resurfaced to discover an important voicemail message – one of the most successful producers in the world was soliciting them. Robert 'Mutt' Lange had performed production honours on AC/DC's *Back In Black* – the second bestselling album of all time. He'd also been involved in Def Leppard's chart-topping albums *Hysteria* and *Pyromania* – something which, for Adam, would instantly place him on a pedestal.

"When I was 10 or 11, I loved Def Leppard," he reminisced. "I was just getting into music and I don't care what anybody says – millions and millions and millions of people love those Def Leppard records. It's fucking Def Leppard! They were like the biggest band in the world at that time."

After reigning over the rock world, Lange had given up his crown to produce the Canadian country singer Shania Twain, who would become his wife. When the pair joined forces on her 1997 album, *Come On Over*, it became the bestselling album by a female artist of all time.

"Mutt Lange is, on paper, one of the most successful record producers of all time," Adam marvelled to *Popeater*. "That's a proven statistic. The guy has written tons of number ones and produced massive, humongous records. Whether you like him or not, those are the facts."

This track record sealed the deal for Maroon 5. By the time he'd contacted them, they'd already sold over 15 million albums worldwide and anyone wanting to join the team on album number three needed credentials to match that mammoth success.

Not only did Lange fit the bill in that regard, he also shared the band's (particularly Jesse's) interest in spiritual enlightenment. He was a follower of the ancient yet little-known group Sant Mat, dating back to 13th-century India, which promoted the principles of egalitarianism. The restrictive Hindu caste system – where birth origin, rather than life achievements, dictated one's standing in society – was rejected and peace had also been promoted between Hindus and Muslims in an era of religious riots. Sant Mat's modern-day aspirations were largely similar to those hundreds of years earlier and the group followed almost Buddhist values.

In keeping with this tradition, Lange lived in privacy and seclusion in a small Swiss town, shunning the city life and working on his music. In the showbiz world, however, where a desperate hunger for publicity often prevailed, his needs would be seen as unorthodox and he'd be labelled as slightly insane.

"It's funny that anyone who basically values their privacy in this day and age is sort of tagged as a recluse," Mickey commented, "but he's one of the most affable, friendly people."

The group would experience his hospitality at first hand when they were invited over for a meeting. "After the initial round of pinching ourselves out of sheer disbelief and googling Mr Lange's name to marvel at his unparalleled track record of musical success extending far beyond the boundaries of genre and era, we were lucky enough to sit down with the man himself," Mickey described. "Having heard the myriad stories of Mutt's obsessive attention to detail and exacting perfectionism, and knowing just how fiercely he protected his privacy over the years in order to maintain an essentially non-existent public image, we were unsure of what to expect – and more than a little intrigued. What none of us had anticipated was the extraordinarily warm, affable low-key guy who arrived, professing an admiration of the band and a humble desire for genuine collaboration to best realise the songs in recorded form. His kind demeanour only made it easier for us to arrive at the conclusion – essentially a foregone one, from the moment Mutt had expressed interest in producing our music – that he was the man for the job."

Within weeks, the band had packed their bags for Switzerland. They arrived at their new producer's sleepy town and shared an apartment directly overlooking a lake – somewhere they would later describe as one of the most scenically beautiful locations they'd ever seen.

"The sheer beauty and pace of our Swiss environs made it easy to clear our heads if we hit a creative wall," Mickey elaborated. "[David] Bowie, [Vladimir] Nabokov, Freddie Mercury, [Charlie] Chaplin and countless other luminaries all spent considerable time in that part of the world and I can see why . . . it is an ideal creative environment. After so much sort of 'short-term' travelling, during which we rarely experience a foreign city for more than a day or two at a time, to live in that tiny Swiss town for three months was a genuine privilege."

Jesse, who'd revealed he had no regrets about failing to graduate from college as a trade-off for success in Maroon 5, certainly didn't view the extended trip as a language-learning opportunity. In fact, he'd memorised just two French phrases to communicate 'please' and 'thank you'. "That's all you need," he insisted – and, as the band voluntarily imprisoned themselves in the studio for up to 14 hours at a time, he'd probably been right.

"We worked seven days a week, 14 hour days," Mickey confirmed. "Mutt and the engineer, they worked even longer hours than that. They are machines. It's mind-blowing . . . leaving LA to record was superproductive."

One of the pluses about the change of scenery was the absence of any kind of schedule and the total lack of distractions. Back in LA, Adam's mind had been speeding at over 100 miles an hour and his phone was constantly ringing with messages from friends hoping to catch him before he left the country yet again. Yet in this rural idyll, he had no choice but to focus purely on music.

"The coolest thing about being in Switzerland was we weren't distracted at all," he explained. "There was nothing to be distracted by, except scenery, which was very beautiful, but once you kind of took all that in, you were left with your own thoughts. It was nice to kind of have that quiet mind, especially for me because I have the hardest time quieting my mind. It was nice having nothing bothering me, nothing on my mind, nothing to do, no obligations. The obligation we had while we were there was to make the best record we possibly could and to kind of dig really deep – and we did."

Removing himself from the LA showbiz circuit also reminded Adam of exactly why he'd needed distance – albeit temporarily – from old haunts such as the Chateau Marmont. Even in those secluded surroundings, he'd been unable to escape from the paparazzi. His fascination with the hotel had taken its first blow when Jessica Simpson innocently emerged from an early morning hairdressing appointment at a salon that happened to be next door to where he was staying, only for the media to report the pair had been having sex there. It was a low-key morning for Jessica, who was wearing minimal make-up and casually dressed, but the media screamed accusations of a dishevelled walk of shame following an all-night sex marathon.

Headlines such as "Jessica Simpson spends night with Maroon 5 Man-whore" had done little to reignite Adam's enthusiasm for the showbiz world. Just weeks before he'd left for Switzerland, yet more rumours had blighted his life.

He'd been snapped on a lunch date at the hotel with a glamorous older woman: film star Cameron Diaz, and her mother Billie. While friends of the band insisted that the meeting had been a pure coincidence that led to a polite lunch, the media interpreted this as serious relationship territory, seeing Adam as obligated to 'meet the parents' for their approval.

As much as he enjoyed socialising with fellow celebrities, Adam had been increasingly realising that work was now his top priority. While the first fruits of success led to self-congratulatory partying, the elation had gradually been overtaken by the pressure of maintaining that level of success – he wouldn't stay at the top long if he got distracted by all the parties.

"I thought, 'I'm going to eat cheeseburgers every day and play poker and go out and have drinks and enjoy myself a little,'" Adam reflected on his more hedonistic Chateau Marmont days, "and I did that and that gets old quickly. Then you get up and realise it's time to start getting serious. I thought, 'OK, let's grow up and focus on making this record amazing!'"

It was that same ambition that had brought him to Switzerland. There would be no paparazzi, no parties and no women – and most refreshingly, no one in these small-town environs seemed to know, or care, who he was.

It was a place to lose his ego – as aided by Mutt Lange who, due to his own longstanding success, was uniquely unimpressed. "He looked at our success as a good start," Adam recalled almost incredulously, "which was really interesting, being in our positions and having someone say, 'All right, that's cute, but you can get there and you're doing good, nice start.' That was a very humbling realisation that we had. He pushed us harder than we've ever been pushed."

Mutt would stretch the group's boundaries, deconstructing and reconstructing songs until they were perfect. An indignant Adam would come into the studio armed with a song he regarded as already finished, only for Mutt – who was not merely a producer but an accomplished songwriter himself – to dismiss it as a good starting point that was still incomplete, telling him to "strip it down to the drums and start over".

This was a new experience for Adam, who was accustomed to having his ego massaged by yes-men – he certainly didn't expect to be continually ordered to produce something better. Yet he was coming up against someone fiercely talented, who was just as much a perfectionist as he was and considered it his duty to push him to the limit.

"Mutt's central thesis behind making records is 'It's got to be the best it can possibly be!'" Adam would admit. "If it's not good enough, make it better. Make it better, always."

While there was potential for a clash of egos – and Adam did initially succumb to a few "really dumb, premature early cock fights", which saw both parties fluctuate from 'I love you' to 'I hate you' – Adam eventually found a way to accept Mutt's input graciously.

"He's a songwriter – the dude writes hit after hit," he acknowledged, "but I said to him, 'Listen, man – in order for this to really be Maroon 5, it has to be written by Maroon 5' – and he was respectful of that. He could easily help us with the writing – there's no doubt. And it took a lot to be able to admit that he could probably help us a lot but that we probably shouldn't take that help because we really needed to do this on our own. He really did respect it. That's why he pushed me even harder, because he had one of his creative hands tied behind his back, basically. So in a weird way, I'm glad he was taking it out on me and forcing me to come up with it."

The pair struck a balance where Adam remained loyal to Maroon 5's style spec, but received unobtrusive and diplomatic guidance from his new musical mentor on how to achieve the sounds he had in mind.

"The relationship was a very valuable one," Adam would admit, "because I've never had a relationship where the guy was coming at it from a songwriting point of view, which was cool because I trusted everything he had to say. The best thing to do is try to check your ego, where you just don't worry about yours versus his. That's always the hardest thing to balance in the studio. You've got five guys, five different opinions, plus a producer and that battle and that wrestling match – which will inevitably take place – is kind of what makes for either a great record or a crappy record!"

Mutt's biggest appeal was that he was working from the heart, purely motivated by a passion for music. At that point in his career, he already had everything he needed – the money, the success and the acclaim – and thus was able to take on projects without any financial motive or vanity.

"He was a really good person to work with because he wasn't one of those guys who was lining up to produce one of our records because they thought maybe they could make a book or it'd be a good thing to be attached to," Adam elaborated. "Mutt doesn't have an agenda. He has millions of dollars and lives in a fantasy land in Switzerland. He's not exactly the kind of guy who really gives a shit about what you can do for him. He's done it all already, so you know his intentions are pure.

"He was tough on me," Adam added thoughtfully, "which was great because no one's ever really been tough on me as far as writing down ideas and saying, 'I don't like this and I don't like that.' He was just a really sweet taskmaster."

Adam had grown tired of adoration and was equally uninterested in fake flattery. He was happy to be taken under the wing of a man who, refreshingly, had no agenda and consequently would be brutally, yet valuably, honest.

As the writing sessions progressed, Mutt guided Adam to succeed where he felt he'd tried but failed on the previous album – in securing the delivery of a trademark Maroon 5 sound that embraced their originality.

"Our first record was a reflection of my love for Stevie Wonder," Adam later reflected. "With the second I kept going back and forth between Prince and the Police. But there was no-one on my mind for this album – it's just great pop."

Yet when it came to the album's title track, 'Hands All Over', Adam admitted to being secretly seduced by the influence of one of Mutt's previous high-profile productions: Def Leppard.

In awe of childhood favourite 'Pour Some Sugar On Me', he would recall admiringly: "It sounded gigantic and the production was huge. The vocals were massive sounding and I just like how it sounded really big . . . bigger than everything else. Even when you heard it for the first time, it sounded like you had already heard it before because it was so massive sounding. I always wanted to achieve that – obviously not the same way, not for the gated reverb drums, all the stuff they used back then, but the bigness, definitely. I think we did achieve that."

Then there was 'Don't Know Nothing', a track which the *Idolator* website described as sounding "like it was ripped straight out of the Motown songbook". "There was a certain period of time when all the best songs were coming out of Motown," Adam would admit. "All the best singers, all the best musicians – James Jamerson, Marvin Gaye, Stevie Wonder, Smokey . . . that was pretty much everybody I worshipped."

However, unlike before, he felt he wasn't emulating the sound of that era but reinterpreting it as his own. "We used to be hellbent on creating a style, a cohesiveness," he added, "but [with the album], the cohesiveness kind of came with the writing. It didn't come with the stylistic choices we made. Whatever it may be, we felt that the thread that was going to tie everything together was going to be the songwriting."

Indeed, there was no clear single style running through the tracks. Slices of sound such as distorted guitars and Adam's ever-present, ever-distinctive vocal were consistent trademarks, but the album did not confine itself to one category. The goal was "not to sound like anyone else" – and the musical diversity helped achieve that.

The overarching theme on the album was still relationships: 'Stutter' spoke of an addiction to an elusive fantasy woman who always seems frustratingly out of reach, while 'I Can't Lie' has Adam abandoning his pride to admit that he's struggling to move on in the aftermath of a break-up. As much as he hates to expose himself to vulnerability – and the loss of dignity that it entails – he has to let his former lover know he's dying a little inside now that she's gone.

'Get Back In My Life' sees Adam's lost pride degenerate a little further in the name of love, as he reduces himself to begging for her to re-ignite the fire that she started. Tightrope walking the fine line between flattering passion and stalker-like obsession, he adds that he will never leave her alone.

'Runaway' shares its name with a Kanye West track, but while the rapper's song is a flippant depiction of being "young, rich and tasteless", Adam's track continues the theme of being desperately but hopelessly in love. He admits he's lost control and ponders whether he's lost that which he needs to survive. The question that replays itself in his head over and over again is why did it all have to end?

'How' sees Adam getting poetic, claiming he has been bound by the shackles of love and wouldn't mind if he died tied up. Yet although he wants the woman who has entwined him to come back, he wonders whether their turbulent history will really allow the possibility.

'Just A Feeling' depicts the awkward ending of a romance, capturing the embitterment of a wronged partner who says she wishes she didn't love him any more. There is a deadness in her eyes as she slowly withdraws and detaches from him, and as he watches the emotion they'd built up evaporate, he intones how he feels it may be the end.

'Give A Little More' sees a wary, once-bitten-twice-shy Adam pledge not to fall in love until his potentially deadly heartbreaker proves her affections and gives as much as he does.

'Out Of Goodbyes', a track created in a single day, is about the need to move on after a toxic affair draws to a close, with country group Lady Antebellum providing guest vocals on the female part of the lyric.

"We really don't know much about the country world," Adam told CNN bluntly, "[but] we heard about this band and their dynamics seemed too right. The harmonies [were] really great. We had them do it from Nashville, which was kind of a long distance studio session. Long distance high-five, Lady Antebellum!"

Then there was 'Never Gonna Leave This Bed', a track penned by Adam in a moment of loneliness and vulnerability after an all-night bender back home in LA. The alcohol loosened his inhibitions, leading him to write honestly about his deep-seated longing for a partner with whom to share his life; the fantasy image he has in mind is of a romance so intoxicating that he quite simply can't be prised out of bed. This demo had originally been recorded in Adam's makeshift shoebox studio at his rented house in LA, but now, with the help of Mutt Lange, he perfected the final version.

The final few recordings comprised bonus tracks for the deluxe edition of the album. 'No Curtain Call' displays Adam taking a confrontational role, determined to succeed. He's ready to see off an enemy, refuses to give up without a fight and vows that he will run straight into the path of a flame rather than run away. While the metaphor of an unwanted curtain call implies not wanting a show – or showdown – to end, it might also be symbolic of not wanting to call time on a relationship. Otherwise, it was the only track on the album not centred on conflict with a woman.

'The Air That I Breathe', meanwhile, depicts a partner who is as important to him as oxygen but who is slowly slipping away as it emerges that it's too late to apologise.

Finally, in 'Last Chance', Adam acknowledges that another man might be able to satisfy his lover's desires for stability and diamond rings, which, due to his touring life and wariness about marriage, he cannot provide. Yet he appeals to her heart by pointing out that, for all his shortcomings, he has one advantage over the safe choice: their extraordinarily strong sexual chemistry. At the same time, he voices the creeping suspicion that it may be his last chance to win her love.

While an album filled entirely with love songs might have entered the realm of cliché in some music fans' eyes, these were no insipid romantic stories – they were always intense, conflicted and twisted. Adam owed much of the emotional intensity and sincerity for which his songwriting was renowned to the fact that he took love seriously. In stark contrast to his rock star/man-whore image, for him affairs were not merely fun or flirtatious – they were obsessive, passionate entanglements of the heart that consumed his soul. The women in his life wounded him and yet, in a masochistic sense, he enjoyed the pain because it inspired such beautiful art – and it was preferable to not having the subject of his desires in his heart at all.

While his penchant for passion in songs had scarcely changed, something else had – for the first time in its history, the band was open to collaborating with other songwriters. While the first two albums had consisted exclusively of band members' input, this time around they'd recruited firm friend Sam Farrar – the bassist in Phantom Planet – to co-write several songs. Meanwhile, the group's tour manager, Shawn Tellez, assisted with penning 'How' and sound engineer Noah Passovoy shared joint honours on 'Runaway'. As difficult as it had been to give others access to their body of material, doing so had brought diversity into the writing process. The fact that they were among trusted friends also made it easier.

As the recording drew to a close, the band took a break from their immersive studio sessions with a European road trip in mind. "We got three motorcycles and a car," Adam later recalled with relish, "and went through the Alps to Italy via France and it was a beautiful motorcycle journey."

"It was one of the most beautiful trips I've taken," Jesse concurred, before adding sardonically of their stop-offs: "I saw lots of rich people spilling champagne and dancing to really horrible music. It was good fun!"

Following their road trip, they returned to the studio to put the finishing touches on the album. It was decided that a live cover version of Alicia Keys' 'If I Ain't Got You' – as well as a live recording of 'Last Chance', which had been a regular fixture on parts of the *It Won't Be Soon Before Long* tour – should be added to the list of bonus tracks. Acoustic versions of songs such as 'Never Gonna Leave This Bed', as well as a rowdy rendition of Queen's 'Crazy Little Thing Called Love', completed the picture.

The final track, 'Misery', lyrically depicted a complicated affair that had recently become unrequited, leaving Adam begging for an end to the silence. "It's about the desperation of wanting someone really badly in your life," he explained to MTV, "but having it be very difficult."

Yet in early 2010, after his return to LA, he would meet someone who would mend his anguish – his first serious relationship since his 2004 separation from Jane. Anne Vyalitsyna – 'Anne V' for short – was a glamorous Victoria's Secret supermodel of Russian origin, seven years his senior.

Anne's career had begun in 2001 at the tender age of 15 – but it couldn't have come a moment too soon for her, as she recalled dreaming of becoming a model "ever since I was little, playing with my Barbie doll". Modelling scouts had caught sight of her long, lean physique on the streets of St. Petersburg while looking for entrants for MTV's *Fashionably Loud Europe* contest – and she needed little persuasion to enter.

She won both the competition and the grand prize of a contract with IMG Models, soon becoming a favourite of *Sports Illustrated* magazine. By the time she met Adam, she had starred in the magazine's industry renowned 'Swimsuit Issue' for six consecutive years and pundits insisted she'd come close to matching predecessor Elle Macpherson's reputation as 'The Body'. She'd also been voted into the Top 10 of the 'Sexiest Supermodels Alive' poll.

To celebrate the release of the 2010 edition of the 'Swimsuit Issue', *Sports Illustrated* was holding a party – and, as its star performers, Maroon 5 were invited. On the day, Adam excitedly blabbed that he loved fashion shows for both the models and the clothes, before hastily correcting himself: "Who am I kidding?! For the models!"

However it wasn't love at first sight for either – when they first laid eyes on one another, both he and Anne were distinctly unimpressed. "He thought I was a stuck-up bitch," his lover-to-be would reveal, "and I kind of thought he was a douche-bag musician!"

In Anne's case, her hesitation might have been justified. After all, despite his best intentions, Adam didn't always come across as a gentleman in print. He'd sounded promiscuous when he mused, "Instinctively, monogamy is not in our genetic make-up" and when, not for the last time, he'd described the withdrawal method as a "fool-proof birth control system", he didn't give the impression that he practised safe sex either. He distinguished himself from those who didn't respect their conquests, however, insisting, "With a lot of guys who are hypersexual, it comes from some sort of disdain or dislike – they're guys who love getting laid but don't really respect women." So far, so good – until he added boast-fully, "That doesn't mean I haven't been totally promiscuous and slutty in my lifetime, because I have."

In a bid to rescue his reputation, he would assert: "There's two kinds of men – there are men who are fucking misogynist pigs and then there are men who just really love women and think they're the most amazing people in the world — and that's me. Maybe the reason I was promiscuous and wanted to sleep with a lot of them is that I loved them so much."

As much as he might have protested his innocence, Anne was seeing red flags. To top it all off, there was his self-confessed mammoth ego, his insatiable desire for attention and his admission that he was "a nightmare" and could never contemplate dating himself.

A needy, self-centred, promiscuous nightmare — on paper, he was America's answer to Russell Brand. One thing was for sure — he was far from the type of man Anne could imagine herself dating. When she met him, she was deliberately aloof, icy and detached, leading Adam to stereotype her as the "stuck-up bitch" she'd spoken of. Yet hate could be as passionate as love, and the two nonetheless noted an inexplicable attraction to one another. By the end of their first meeting, to the astonishment of both parties, they'd found themselves exchanging phone numbers. It was the beginning of an intense affair.

The pairing of a model and a musician was, in the eyes of many, the oldest cliché in the book — and yet there was much controversy surrounding their relationship due to Adam's previous comments about Anne's body type. At the time it began, the use of implausibly thin models on the catwalk was a hot topic. Health campaigners felt it was impossible for most women to safely achieve the weight of their style idols, but the trend for 'size zero' was encouraging young and impressionable followers of fashion to starve themselves to achieve the same desired jeans size.

While a minority of women might have been extraordinarily small-boned, with an unusually narrow pelvis and small bra size, the reality was that a typically feminine figure was the polar opposite of many catwalk models. Yet 'heroin chic' — the nineties term for a deliberately pale, emaciated and unhealthy demeanour — remained an on-trend look in high fashion and, as models struggled to achieve this counter-intuitive ideal, stories spread of them fainting backstage or, in a few cases, even dying of heart failure.

Despite some half-hearted promises within the industry to no longer use 'underweight' models, many critics suspected that the *Vogue* definition of the term might not match that of the medical profession. As it was, the average supermodel tended to don clothes around five sizes smaller than the average in the general population.

While most of Anne's modelling assignments – commissions from the likes of *Sports Illustrated* and lingerie giant Victoria's Secret – had a sexier feel than those of the average supermodel and therefore meant a very slightly fleshier look, the pressure to be unnaturally thin remained overwhelming. In fact, one of her Victoria's Secret peers would later publish an exposé on the culture at the lingerie house, entitled *I'm No Angel: From Victoria's Secret Model To Role Model*.

The book detailed author Kylie Bisutti's "personal struggles with inadequacy, low self-esteem and her near constant quest for approval in a world where you can never be thin enough, pretty enough or sexy enough".

"I pretty much restricted my diet to oatmeal, fruits and vegetables to meet runway expectations," she would reveal. "I'm five feet ten and I got down to 115 pounds [but] while everyone I knew was being sent out to auditions, I wasn't. 'Why am I still going on test shoots?' I asked my agent. 'It's because you look like a fat cow, Kylie. You need to lose two inches off your hips,' the agent said. After cutting my diet even further to just pineapples, watermelons and litres of water . . . I finally dropped down to 108 pounds, which satisfied my agent and the gigs started rolling in."

Of course, reaching these proportions was far from easy. In fact, Bisutti would add of one of her flatmates, "She was so bulimic she would involuntarily throw up when she ate. She would go to sleep crying every night and just look at herself in the mirror thinking that she was so fat – and she was so thin."

According to Kylie's exposé, the Victoria's Secret girls she knew had been universally and desperately unhappy, suffering a deep guilt in their relationship with food – so much so that the hunger pangs were almost bearable in contrast to the revulsion they felt at giving in to them. The quote that best summed up how Kylie experienced life as a Victoria's Secret model was, "I felt like a piece of meat."

Perhaps that might be more accurately described as a piece of bone. As Anne herself would confess, "There is a certain weight I feel comfortable in. The thing is, with *Sports Illustrated*, they want the whole voluptuous, soft body – sometimes I'm not comfortable with that."

Her comments supported Kylie's story of a culture that placed increasing pressure on models to lose weight. Yet while Adam had begun to date her, he'd previously seemed scornful of girls like Anne and all that they represented.

"The size zero thing is sad," he'd asserted in one interview. "I wish women wouldn't do it. Men like flesh. They like women to have the curves they're supposed to have. The whole situation is more about women competing with other women than about women's sexual appeal to men. I have yet to meet a man who says, 'I love a woman who's all skin and bones.'"

Yet despite being adamant that size zero was unattractive, Adam had now started dating a model of exactly that size – and she wouldn't be the last one for him. It all seemed to date back to his teenage fantasies, most of which had revolved around having a model on his arm.

"I imagined it around 4 p.m. when I got back from school every day – very vividly, in fact," an animated Adam recalled of his obsession. "Victoria's Secret was the Bible for a young adolescent boy. All we had was that or the Sunday paper. There was slim pickings back in the day for our stimulation."

For him perhaps, dating Anne was the real-life enactment of those teenage clichés, reminding him of the first stirrings of sexual excitement. Yet while, in the absence of anything more pornographic, the Victoria's Secret girls had been the earliest sexual obsessions of his youth, most of the models had matched the size-zero criteria he'd spoken out against. According to Adam, Anne's body type was not only less than desirable, it was even immoral – and yet, in spite of the openness of that opinion, he'd started dating her. While the gaping contradiction between his words and his actions might have made for an awkward romance, Adam had nonetheless fallen hard.

"This is the most functional relationship I've ever been in," he told the media earnestly. "I don't want to screw it up."

He demonstrated his commitment to Anne by featuring her in the video for 'Misery' – the debut single from *Hands All Over*. It began with Adam falling forcefully to the ground after being pushed over the edge of a building by his lover. It might have been interpreted as a middle-finger salute to those who accused him of misogyny in 'Wake Up Call', as this time he'd reversed the gender roles and turned the anger on himself.

"It turns the whole idea of the sexual energy between two people – a guy and a girl, a music video, you've seen that a million times – that exists in this video, but it's turning it on its ass and having the girl be the more domineering one who's trying to kill me," Adam announced to MTV.

Sparking rumours of a sadomasochistic relationship between Adam and Anne, played out for the public in exhibitionistic style through the particularly violent video, she projected the image of a dangerous lover. Caressing her face with a knife, she proceeds to punch him, kick him painfully in the nether regions, perform a water-boarding ritual on him in a public toilet, push him into oncoming traffic and, of course, to send him flying from atop a dizzyingly tall building. By the final frame – when he falls limply to the ground, his microphone beside him – his over-enthusiastic lover has seemingly killed him off. Switching from a kiss to a punch at lightning-fast speed, the plot captured the often intensely volatile nature of passion.

Bizarrely, Adam seemed to love every minute of his demise, animatedly telling an MTV crew on the day of filming, "I just had my first harness experience. That was very interesting. I got lowered onto the street in the middle of traffic because I fell off a building . . . I've already been beaten up and thrown off a building today, we'll have to see what comes next."

Of course, for the most dangerous parts of the video, stuntmen were hired. Adam's most difficult role involved being dangled six feet in the air from a crane before careful lowering onto the choreographed scene of a traffic-filled road – and that was heart-pounding enough. To maximise the impact, his stunt double had to perform the same moves but from a much higher drop. Every bit as macho as one might expect men who'd chosen such a dangerous profession to be, the stunt team didn't take kindly to the necessity of donning the band's fashionably androgynous clothes.

"The stuntmen were so great, but they probably weren't too happy because they had to dress like us!" Adam chortled. "[It] was hilarious because we aren't the most masculine dressers! This dude who was Jesse's stunt-double was, like, really buff, and he has Jesse's little low-top Converse and skinny jeans on. The shoes were, like, falling off his massive ankles!"

Anne, who'd previously appeared in the 2004 Alanis Morissette video 'Out Is Through,' got a warm reception from viewers, while the eye-catchingly realistic violence guaranteed the mini-movie a place on every major music channel's playlist. The single would eventually peak at number 14 on the *Billboard* chart.

Meanwhile, although macho men may have mocked his wardrobe – and doubtless his penchant for styling Rihanna, if they'd known – Adam's intuitive relationship with fashion was about to become a highly lucrative side project for him.

He'd always relished flashy clothes, though there'd been times in his teens when he'd momentarily despised them. "One summer I got grounded for throwing a party on the roof of our apartment," Adam explained. "As a punishment I had to work in my dad's warehouse all summer ticketing shoulder pads . . . it was back in the early nineties, so shoulder pads were still around. I had to ticket boxes of them for about eight weeks!"

Yet as much as he might have cursed the incident, it hadn't permanently soured his relationship with style. In fact, when he hit the limelight as the lead singer of Maroon 5, he'd positively revelled in it.

"I went through a very un-casual phase," he revealed. "My nose would be turned up and I would insist on wearing the best of the best. I would go to dinner in ties and jackets and Balenciaga and stuff. I got caught up in the whole idea of fashion and the Margielas and Anne Demeulemeesters of the world. There's a real art behind that . . . it's a beautiful, amazing world."

The one and only time he had clashed with Kanye West was when the latter had worn an exquisitely tailored, white corduroy YSL blazer to an awards ceremony – coincidentally the same as one Adam had just bought, leaving him reluctant to wear it in public lest he was branded a copycat.

As his interest in style grew, it seemed the right time to collaborate with his father and other family members on a clothing line of his own – one which he would christen 222, in honour of his lucky number and the Hollywood recording studio from his early years that had inspired it.

Ironically, for someone who had coveted designer brands and retrospectively described himself as a "label whore", Adam's line was to be minimalistic and budget-conscious – the polar opposite of his attitude earlier in his career.

"It wasn't really me," he would admit by way of explanation, writing off an entire era of performing in expensive suits as an eccentric phase. "Before all this nonsense, I was touring in a van with jeans and a ripped

T-shirt and a leather jacket if I could afford it – and that's what got me through to where I am today."

Consequently, his line consisted of a series of understated jeans, T-shirts and jackets, while his additional women's range included casual knitted tops and wraps. The most expensive item in the line was a $1,250 biker jacket that channelled classic film icons such as Marlon Brando and James Dean, while T-shirts retailed at just $30 – almost modest by rock star standards.

"It's very simple and pure and durable," he reiterated. "Jeans, T-shirts and a leather jacket – that's all I need. I think it's always fun to be the most under-dressed person in a room. There will be no bedazzling in this collection. I like subtlety in design. These days, so much stuff looks like someone vomited over it."

He would even suggest his penchant for expensive labels was a weakness rather than a plus, commenting wryly, "When you sell [millions of] albums and the money starts to come in, it does things to you that you either recover from or don't!"

While this stance was about as far from the Adam of old as it was possible to be, the clothing line showcased his maturity and growth in recent years, as well as his interest in going back to basics and reacquainting himself with his down-to-earth, pre-fame self. Yet he couldn't revert to his pre-fame schedules and, with regret, found himself leaving much of his promotional duties to his long-time stylist, Aristotle Circa, his father's cousin, Sami Cooper, who owned the clothes manufacturing company that produced the line, and of course his father himself, with all the retail industry experience he had to share.

"I always had a profound respect for my dad's business and his success," Adam would continue, "[although] I was never interested in being a part of it. I had tunnel vision for music. But [then] I thought about combining our two talents and interests. It was kind of synergistic. It feels very natural – it's a no-brainer."

The launch took place in Las Vegas, in August 2010, but again with minimal involvement from Adam, other than his intensive input and collaboration behind the scenes. In fact there was a good reason – other than timing constraints – why he'd stepped back from it in public.

"I want the line to be successful on its own merit," he explained. "I would love for it to be successful without my celebrity playing into it."

However, even a celebrity name attached to a line didn't instantly guarantee its future. That summer, Madonna and her daughter, Lourdes, had launched their own range, Material Girl, to an atmosphere of indifference from critics and apparel-buying public alike. Yet while Madonna's line was dubbed 'passé' and 'underwhelming', and underperformed financially, Adam's back-to-basics approach would prove extremely popular.

While the fashion line went from strength to strength, Adam returned to the touring circuit to promote the album's second single, 'Give A Little More', which made its debut as a digital download on August 17. It would follow into mainstream radio two months later. Unfortunately, it wasn't as much of a hit as expected – its grainy video, featuring a simulation of a house party, gradually fell away from music channel playlists and the track failed to even make it to the Top 40 on the *Billboard* chart. (The only territory in which it claimed the top spot was South Korea.)

That stroke of misfortune continued to haunt the band when the album was released on September 21. First-week sales were more than three times lower than the previous album and, after that crucial introductory week, its popularity dropped sharply. While sales would reach the 500,000 mark within a couple of months – an undisputed cause for celebration for most artists – Maroon 5's expectations had been higher, leaving them deflated and anxious to record new material as early as possible.

However, for one surprised contributor the album surpassed all of her expectations. In keeping with Adam's new back-to-basics approach, instead of commissioning a high-profile celebrity photographer, the band used a cover image that British teenager Rosie Hardy happened to have shared on Flickr.

"I'd named that picture 'I need to feel your hands all over me', which was a lyric from a song I liked at the time," she explained. "The band's management saw it and contacted me about possibly remaking it to fit the image the guys had in mind – slightly more sexual, with some real va-va-voom to it. At first I thought it was a scam, but I followed it through anyway and before I knew it we were putting together the final touches for their album!"

She'd shot the iconic frames in her bedroom, featuring her own naked torso. "It was just a case of putting together different poses and combining the hands afterwards in the editing," she recalled, before adding blushingly, "I don't think any of my neighbours saw me gallivanting around the room – at least I hope not!"

While the group had been looking for an erotic image with multiple hands clasping a body, as if they were faceless members of an orgy, Rosie's more sentimental interpretation also resonated. "The image represents memories, sadness at leaving somebody behind and a fire that an old flame will leave and one that you're never entirely sure will burn out," she mused.

★ ★ ★

By October 2010, Adam was lending his name to the It Gets Better campaign, a video project devised by columnist Dan Savage in support of lesbian, gay, bisexual and transsexual lifestyles. He'd started it in response to a string of suicides driven by homophobic bullying – in particular, that of tragic Billy Lucas, who'd been just 15 at the time. These tragedies made a good argument for educating children in their primary school years that homosexuality was a valid lifestyle choice, effectively normal for a minority – something to be accepted instead of mocked. Yet while education might have normalised the concept and removed the temptation to tease – or worse – some members of society, especially Republican voters, believed that such a move would 'promote' gay lifestyles and was therefore inherently immoral. Challenging the stereotypes and preconceptions of an intolerant majority was a huge undertaking – with that problem in mind, Savage had decided to start by sending a message of positivity directly to the victims: "It gets better."

To Adam's surprise, he had been approached to take part not by Dan himself but by another contributor, gay celebrity blogger Perez Hilton. "I found it strange that one of the biggest bullies on Earth is asking me," mused an incredulous Adam. "I thought he was part of the problem."

Indeed, Perez had built his reputation – and it was a formidable one, at times reputedly netting millions of visitors to his website per day – on poking fun at celebrities for the public's entertainment. He would publish photos of people with obscenities he'd scrawled across their faces. He'd published shots taken up the skirts of then-underage teenage girls such as Miley Cyrus, in an apparent bid to embarrass and humiliate them, as well as to increase his site's viewing figures. He'd outed celebrities such as Neil Patrick Harris and N-Sync's Lance Bass as gay, without their consent or knowledge. He'd nicknamed actress Jennifer Aniston 'Maniston'. He'd offended Fergie so much that, in 2006, she'd written the song 'Pedestal' as a reaction to his insults. In lyrically accusing her tormentor of feeling that it was acceptable to tear down public figures due to their status, she hit the nail on the head.

For Perez, nothing was out of bounds – he justified his intrusive and often malicious coverage by insisting celebrities had chosen to become famous and that, without writers like him to promote them, they would have long since faded into obscurity. Bizarrely, the openly gay blogger would even allegedly regale Fergie's Black Eyed Peas bandmate, rapper Will.i.am, a straight man, with an anti-gay slur during a heavily documented altercation out on the town.

Yet when he was invited to change his ways and be part of It Gets Better, the cause seemed to strike a chord with Perez – and he vowed to turn his reputation around by stopping the online bullying of celebrities.

"I have been doing everything I can to bring awareness to the issue of teen suicides and gay bullying," he claimed. "In doing so, a lot of people have called me a hypocrite and a bully myself . . . it was a big wake-up call that so many people saw me that way, so from now I really want to be part of the solution and not part of the problem."

To demonstrate his commitment, he'd posted a video on YouTube titled 'I'm Going To Be Doing Things Differently'. Viewers might have taken his pledge more seriously if he hadn't used the opportunity for yet more self-promotion, prominently name-checking three new websites he was launching. However, he'd made his promise and, as part of it, had recruited Adam.

"I was hoping to see a change in him and I saw one," Adam would reason. "The guy has changed his tune quite a bit. I respect that."

As for his own contribution to the video project, Adam briefly shared his own experiences of being bullied in high school. "People are really brutal and horrible to each other," he mused, "and we've all been there and have experienced it and it leads to people doing horrible things." He added encouragingly, "I hated high school. High school fucking sucks, but if you can get through it, there is a whole world beyond just people treating you badly . . . please don't let them win, it's such a terrible energy to spread and all I can say is, as the project says, it gets better."

The month after the video was released, Jesse played his own part in publicising gay rights when he blogged his top reasons for voting Democrat instead of Republican. Like Adam, he objected to the Republican plans to keep the 'Don't Ask, Don't Tell' policy, which forbade openly homosexual men and women from serving in the military, pointing out the Democrats planned to repeal the law. He also objected to the policy of some Republican candidates to the federal regulation of businesses; if restaurants were able to withdraw from regulation, for example, he worried some might choose to reverse the compulsory law that insisted all restaurants serve African-Americans.

Other concerns included the widespread Republican belief that climate change legislation was unnecessary because global warming was neither a significant issue nor a manmade crisis. In contrast, the Democratic policy was to invest heavily in renewable energy such as solar, wind, geothermal and tidal power, looking upon them as a long-term investment for the future. Democrats also sought to limit how much of taxpayers' money could be spent on political campaigning at election time.

The band would use a few of their shows to emphasise these political issues, too. The concerts this time around were also enhanced by the addition of multifaceted musician, writer and performer PJ Morgan, who took on joint keyboard duties with Jesse and added his tones to backing vocals.

The following year, 2011, brought the new single, 'Never Gonna Leave This Bed'. The video once again featured Adam's beau, Anne, as the pair reclined on various impromptu bed setups, sometimes in very public places. While one bed was in the not-so-unusual location of the LA Hilton hotel, another was in the middle of Broadway and a third was at a pier on Santa Monica beach. Unsurprisingly, passers-by would gawp at them with a mixture of curiosity and confusion, some even stopping to snap photos.

While it peaked at a disappointing number 55 in the USA, sparking fears that Maroon 5's popularity was waning, their next single would prove otherwise. In fact, it would become their biggest hit yet.

9

Overexposed

THE first step to that career-changing single was enrolling on brand new TV show *The Voice*. On paper, however, Adam's endorsement seemed about as probable as him shunning Stevie Wonder. He'd already publicly registered his contempt for the much-despised genre of reality TV, groaning, "I accept the fact that there are real housewives out there, but I don't need to watch a fucking television show about it" – and according to him, singing contests fitted that same category. "I scoffed at [*The Voice*] initially," he explained. "It's just a bunch of fucking assholes who are fame whores."

Not only did he feel that producers, audiences and reality stars alike rated sex appeal, scandal and often downright stupidity above talent, he also felt that so-called singing competitions made a mockery of their contestants. The emphasis was all too often on poking fun at deluded hopefuls – many of whom were ear-splittingly tuneless. On one occasion, he'd seen a woman with transparent mental health issues warbling incoherently into the microphone to a tirade of jeers, boos and hysterical laughter – it was ratings gold at someone else's expense. Just as, centuries earlier, the public had flocked to Bedlam to jeer at the mentally unstable for entertainment, the modern generation was resorting to reality TV to get its fix of freaks – and in Adam's eyes, it was morally repugnant.

Yet NBC was poised to convince him that *The Voice* was different. Dispensing with the gimmicks, this show would pride itself on its purely vocal focus. To guarantee that no prejudice came into play, judges would be faced away from contestants, pressing a button to swivel their chair around only if they liked what they heard. This move was a reaction against the nation's image-obsessed culture, with singers on rival shows such as *The X*

Factor, *American Idol* and *America's Got Talent* frequently suspected of being chosen on looks alone, in spite of mediocre voices. *The Voice's* approach also staved off the temptation to be seduced by sob stories or novelty acts – something for which other shows were renowned.

This eased Adam's conscience a little – which was just as well as, for both himself and NBC, desperate times called for desperate measures. NBC's ratings had hit an all-time low and four programming chiefs had come and gone in as many years, each having pioneered a failed bid to revive the channel's reputation. NBC was in the Last Chance Saloon when it took on *The Voice* at the elevated sum of $2.3 million per episode, a figure which made it the most expensive unscripted show in its history. The programming bosses were relying on the show to turn their ill fortune around and, with a large portion of the expenses comprising judges' pay cheques, they clearly had faith in Adam's ability to be a part of that transformation.

Meanwhile, Maroon 5 was also at a crossroads. *Hands All Over* had undoubtedly been a commercial disappointment and, with extraordinary candour, Adam admitted that he'd ultimately chosen to take part in the show to inject some life into his own career – one he'd feared was failing.

"Honestly, the risk-reward situation was such that we thought it would be better for me by doing it," he'd recall, "because the band was, I wouldn't say faltering, but not doing as well at that point as we wanted to be doing."

When Cee Lo Green, who was known as a credible artist rather than merely a hot celebrity, signed up for the show, it soothed Adam's fears still further. He would also be joined by the formidable Christina Aguilera and equally successful country star Blake Shelton – and, to allow all four to bond before the show, executive producer Mark Burnett decided to add to the channel's already enormous bill and send the judges out on the town with his American Express card.

"It was important for them to go out socially and I didn't want producers there," he insisted, before acknowledging, "Can you think of a crazier idea than giving four music stars your credit card and drivers and sending them out to the Soho House? I remember Adam saw me the next day and said, 'Dude, that was such a mistake. Wait until you see your American Express bill.'"

In an unrepentant Burnett's eyes, whether their drunken night out ended in catfights or kisses, the chemistry between judges was "absolutely crucial to the show's success". And perhaps he was on to something, because *The Voice* would prove to be an indisputable success, saving NBC from yet another year in the ratings basement.

That inaugural season, which began in April 2011 and pulled in an average of over 12 million viewers per episode, gave NBC a first place finish among the much sought after 18 to 49 demographic. Crucially the show's success allowed Adam an opportunity to redefine his reputation.

"No one knew what I was really like or whether I had anything to say," he argued, before adding wryly, "I think that the occasional soccer mom probably thought I was a slut."

With a back catalogue of comments such as, "Legs, I'm a fan of legs. That's gone away. The question nowadays is always, are you an ass man? Legs are a long lost old school thing. People forget about legs. Legs are important," perhaps it was hardly surprising he'd been misunderstood.

"I've always felt a little misrepresented in the world," he continued. "I felt like people only knew me as a singer who dated pretty girls. A little bit of a bimbo. I was the music dude that was naked all the time with the girls and that's fine, no problem with that, but I wanted to create a little balance. When the show came around, I thought, 'People know now that I have a brain.'"

According to Adam, the public's low expectations of the average pop star pin-up's brain power would work to his advantage. "As a pop star, you don't have to be that smart for people to think you're intelligent," he joked. "The bar is fucking low – if you have half a brain, they think you're amazing – so I have that going for me."

Later, while NBC's president, Paul Telegdy, joked that he would go crazy if he was compelled to hear any more about Adam's "beautifully tattooed, python-like forearms" – and he did accumulate a fanbase tuning in for precisely that reason – Adam also was able to display previously unknown skills at judging and mentoring.

"I'd hate to characterise Adam as man candy," Telegdy asserted, "because he's much more than that. He's extremely talented, hilariously funny and he's got that naughty boy quality about him."

When the show aired, Christina had been seen as the unrivalled star, pulling in the celebrity-watching crowd, while Adam was merely the failing rock star trying to preserve a rapidly crumbling career. Yet the tables quickly turned, with Adam becoming the breakout favourite. According to one marketing firm's research, public awareness of Adam tripled after joining the show, while his likability increased by 20 per cent. The statistics supported these claims too – at one stage in the show's cycle, @AdamLevine received 2.14 million mentions on Twitter, outscoring all the other coaches.

The only danger of Adam's newfound success was the unspoken threat that it might change the dynamic in Maroon 5. He'd sworn that he'd never become a solo artist because he loved the camaraderie of touring with his 'bros'.

He'd also questioned the authenticity of breaking away from a winning formula. "Look at a band like U2 that's been around forever – I'm not sure how people would react to a record called *Bono*," he'd reasoned. "I don't ever want to be that person. It's much cooler to be in a band."

But did his stint on *The Voice* mean sacrificing the goodwill within the band, now that his fame as an individual overshadowed all that he'd done with the group? James, who'd noted that Adam had "lead singer disease", admitted to refusing even to watch his primetime TV slots in the beginning. "I don't need to turn on the TV to hear Adam's opinions," he claimed. "That's not entertainment for me."

As bewildered and ambivalent as the others may have felt at being left behind, while Adam suddenly appeared on every billboard, they gradually became acclimatised to it – even tuning in to show their support.

"When I finally caught it, I got hooked like everyone else," James would later admit, adding laughingly, "Now I find myself yelling at the TV, 'Turn your chair around, Adam! If you don't, that guy's kids won't have health insurance!'"

During a pow-wow with the rest of the group, Adam clarified that he was stepping into the limelight not to satisfy his own ego, but for Maroon 5. He'd been convinced that his gig at *The Voice* would further their profile collectively – and he wasn't wrong.

The chain of events that would lead to the group's revival started with a chance request to become involved in rap-rock group Gym Class Heroes' single 'Stereo Hearts'. The song's intertwined themes were romance and music, and Adam would sing on the chorus that his heart was a stereo which played its beats for a lover. The collaboration, despite achieving respectable Top 5 chart positions in both the USA and the UK, would just be a footnote in Adam's career – but a songwriter he met while recording it would change Maroon 5's direction forever.

The group had historically been reluctant to work with songwriters, shunning them altogether on the first two albums and recruiting them from within their inner circle on the third. They'd been against disrupting or diluting their organic trademark sound by deferring to others' ideas of the most lucrative sonic trend. Yet Benny Blanco, the writer and producer who approached Adam to sing on 'Stereo Hearts', was worth breaking the mould for.

"The experience was so positive and productive that it opened us up to the idea of collaborating with outside writers, a concept that we as a band had always dismissed," Mickey would recall. "The idea of having a fresh perspective on our music and our sound, however, began to really appeal to us after 10 years of working in more or less the same mould. During the session for 'Stereo Hearts', Benny played for Adam a song he had been holding on to, mostly composed by Swedish whiz-kid Shellback, called 'Moves Like Jagger'. The irreverence, sheer danceability and pure catchiness of the song hit us hard. After some spirited debate within the band about the wisdom of working with outside composers and making something so unabashedly 'pop', the 'ayes' won out."

With Blanco on board – a man responsible for a string of *Billboard* number one singles – they were almost guaranteed a hit. His hit list already included Katy Perry's 'Teenage Dream' and 'California Gurls', Britney Spears' 'Circus', Taio Cruz's 'Dynamite' and Ke$ha's 'Tik Tok' – all songs that had become virtual household names.

To top it all off, he'd been just 21 when Maroon 5 first met him. "It's almost as if he has the Midas touch," an incredulous Adam marvelled.

Even better, Benny Blanco had nailed the paradox of achieving mainstream hits by totally unconventional means. He'd written and recorded parts of the multi-million selling 'Tik Tok' on a $25 children's keyboard so old that the keys were grubby, yellowed and uneven. "I don't care if it sounds bad," he'd famously remarked. "I just want to sound different than anyone else."

As unusual as his ethos was, it worked every time – and 'Moves Like Jagger' was no exception. Meanwhile, the band's link with *The Voice* and the friendship Adam had forged with Christina Aguilera opened the door for them to invite her onto the single – and she accepted.

"We wanted a female perspective and Christina is an incredible singer," Adam reasoned. "We'd been sitting next to each other every day on *The Voice* so it made sense."

Upon its June 21, 2011, release it became Maroon 5's first Top 10 chart debut in four years. It would continue to rise until it reached the top spot in 16 countries, eventually becoming the eighth bestselling digital single of all time, with over 10 million copies sold.

In Adam's eyes, its success was due in no small part to the archive footage of the song's muse, Mick Jagger himself, on the video. While older music fans would remember his notoriety from the sixties and seventies, the younger generation were being introduced to the icon for the first time. The Rolling Stones had certainly made a profound impact on Adam as he grew up, and he'd later confess that their onstage prowess had intimidated him into rethinking his entire approach.

"I remember watching an old Stones live show once and the energy was beyond belief," he recalled. "I thought, 'What the hell have I been doing? This is bullshit. I'm bullshit.' That's when I realised I needed to create that much energy when I play."

Emulating the Stones' frontman – not to mention name-checking him in a song – had clearly paid off. "That song pumped new life into our group," Adam acknowledged. "We needed it, because we were struggling. I'm not going to lie. The sales of our third album were a letdown. Making that record had been a struggle, but then 'Moves Like Jagger' lit a fire under us all."

In fact, the single had such a high profile that Jagger would make it a point of reference when he appeared on *The Late Show With David Letterman*, to give his definitive list of 'The Top 10 Things I, Mick Jagger, Have Learned After 50 Years In Rock'n'Roll': "You don't earn a cent when someone does a song called 'Moves Like Jagger'."

Yet the track was testament to Mick's astonishing longevity – he was not merely historically significant, but he was also a relevant part of contemporary culture – even recording vocals for a song with Will.i.am and

J-Lo. Despite all the years that had passed, younger established vocalists aspired to emulate him.

"Do I really have moves like Jagger? Fucking hell, no I don't," Adam pre-emptively retorted. "But I was going to tell everybody that I did and hoped they believe me."

Otherwise, Adam remained unswervingly honest – and often provocatively so. Emboldened by his increasing success, he didn't hesitate to say exactly what he saw. "I don't lie and that's unusual in a world of media-obsessed, media-trained fucking liars who will sit here with you and totally bullshit you to further their own careers," he raged. "I say the wrong thing, I offend people and I piss people off – all of which I like."

Indeed, diplomacy was not a word in the Levine dictionary. One such example of that was when, with defiant disregard for the ceremony's role in awarding him a trophy seven years earlier, he lashed out publicly at the Video Music Awards and the music channel that hosted them.

"The VMAs – one day a year when MTV pretends to still care about music," he tweeted. "I'm drawing a line in the sand. Fuck you, VMAs." He was referring to the channel's large amount of programming unrelated to music. MTV tweeted back its own sarcastic response, referring to the VMA trophy he'd previously won in the shape of an astronaut planting an MTV flag in space:

"Sooo you'll be tuning in at 9/8C tomorrow, right? (BTW, bonus points if you TwitPic your 2004 Moonman!)"

However Adam had the last triumphant word in the exchange: "Still waiting to have my Jerry Maguire mission statement moment of deep regret – not happening. Phew!"

This devil-may-care attitude demonstrated Adam's evolution as an artist via *The Voice*. He'd reached the ultimate pinnacle of self-confidence, no longer paying lip service to corporate bodies he didn't believe in, in a bid to secure their publicity or favour. He now had a platform of his own to address the USA every week, enabling him to dispense with the restrained diplomacy to which more manufactured groups were tied and pursue success on his own terms in a way that allowed him to remain true to himself.

His next major moment of candour came just two months later, when he delivered an all-too-clear message to one of America's most popular news networks: "Dear Fox News, don't play our music on your evil fucking channel ever again – thank you," he tweeted.

The channel's hosts gave as good as they got. One hit back, "Dear Adam, that's not music", while another added: "Dear Adam Levine, don't make crappy fucking music ever again. Thank you!"

However, there was far more to Adam's objection than met the eye. While his critics instantly seized upon it as an arrogant, diva-style tantrum, his views were in fact political in nature. In 2009, *American Idol* runner-up Adam Lambert had made the admission that he'd wanted to come out as gay during the competition, but had been intimidated into not doing so by the advice of Fox.

"It was hard for me because I wasn't able to talk," he'd recall. "So I was sitting there going, 'I can't really put in my two cents.' It felt out of control and feeling out of control is scary."

The network was renowned for its conservative ethos and Republican stance; additionally, it might have felt that homophobic prejudice among viewers could hinder Lambert's chances of progressing in the contest.

Yet for Adam, in the 21st century that was unacceptable. "What's always pissed me off about *Idol* is wanting to mask that, for that to go unspoken," he claimed disapprovingly. "C'mon. You can't be publicly gay? At this point? On a singing competition? Give me a break. You can't hide basic components of these people's lives. The fact that *The Voice* didn't have any qualms about being completely about [the voice itself] is a great thing."

With cheerful disregard for his record label's blushes, Adam would also extend his honesty to the material he performed. The commonly accepted view was that someone's integrity as a live performer rested upon their loyalty to the music, but Adam countered that simply: "I don't like enough of the songs that much. There's only a few that I get really attached to and the rest of it all becomes kind of middle ground for me."

There was another reason for his lack of diplomacy – the band hoped that their days at the label were numbered, meaning that they no longer had an incentive to 'play the game'.

"We desperately want to get out of our record deal," Adam casually revealed to *Entertainment Weekly*. "We want to be free, to make our own records on our own label. It's what every band really wants to do."

In the past, the band had appreciated the advice, support and financial backing offered by Octone, and wouldn't have thought of going it alone. But as they'd evolved as a group, and as their financial power increased, they'd begun to crave creative control and autonomy.

The clock was ticking – with Adam's success on *The Voice* positioning the group at an all-time peak, there couldn't have been a better time to go it alone. Yet they were contractually obligated to fulfil a four-album deal with Octone before they would be free to pursue their dream of autonomy. To speed up the process, for the first time ever they started recording a fourth album while they were still touring the third. Feeling they needed to capitalise on Adam's heightened profile as quickly as possible, they resolved to follow in the footsteps of 'Moves Like Jagger' by recruiting outside songwriters.

"What was happening with *The Voice*, it felt like a moment we should take advantage of," Adam elaborated. "We didn't want to rest on our laurels. We'd made three records in 10 years. Knowing ourselves and that we get too fucking involved, working with outside writers and producers was going to make it work in the time frame we needed it to work."

Yet the decision sparked some insecurity amongst the band members. "I was territorial at first," James confessed. "Like, 'Who are these guys and what's my place in this gonna be now?'"

The other curveball was personal musical preferences: Matt's background lent itself to a more alternative sound; he'd despised the commercial tones of 'Moves Like Jagger' and was concerned that the pop direction in which Maroon 5 was heading was the wrong one – though it was also indisputably the most lucrative.

Thus, while Matt saw the move to catchy dance beats as a concession to popular culture, a form of selling their souls, the others simply regarded it as an essential part of trying to adapt, evolve and remain relevant on the modern music scene. It was a survival of the fittest scenario, with just two options – evolve or die.

In the wake of the disappointing reception to their previous album, Maroon 5 couldn't risk allowing the latter. "The price of admission is that there is a sound you have to slot into, if you even want a shot on radio," James commented. "Whether that's good or bad is another discussion, but that's the way it's been for the last two years."

The popular genres of choice had shifted since the nineties from rock to bubblegum pop, dance-pop and mainstream R&B – but in Adam's view, vocalists had needed to adapt their sound throughout musical history. "Look at every major artist during the disco era from the Rolling Stones to Rod Stewart to Abba!" he remarked. "They were trying to fit in!"

The decision to recruit 'Moves Like Jagger' writers Benny Blanco and Shellback a second time running was an obvious one – they'd already proved themselves by taking the group to number one. Maroon 5 also brought to the party, among others, pop tunesmith extraordinaire Max Martin – someone whose back catalogue included work with Katy Perry, Christina Aguilera and Britney Spears.

"Max is like the elder statesman of pop music and we felt like he could wrangle all the staff writers and producers," Adam revealed. "It made sense for him to be at the helm" – though in fact he co-wrote and co-produced a total of two tracks for the album.

Of course, the experience was initially intimidating. "Sometimes a co-writer will write something that's almost better than what you would do and it's like, 'Shit!'" Adam admitted. "Up to now, we've been insulated from the pop-industrial complex. We've been like, 'Fuck you, we're a band.' But now, stepping into this new world of songwriters and producers, it feels fun."

The songwriters would also help guide the material in one unified direction – the lack of which, the band now felt, had been a fatal flaw on their last album. They'd originally been proud of its diversity and refusal to be pigeonholed, citing their peaceful Swiss surrounds as an inspiration for their best material yet; since then, however, due to the CD's poor commercial performance they'd changed their stance.

"I don't think we knew what kind of a record we were making," Adam retrospectively criticised, in conversation with the *Los Angeles Times*. "It was such a hotchpotch of all these disparate ideas and songs that didn't make any sense together. We were in this idyllic paradise, which is a horrible place to make a record. Switzerland's neutrality is very famous and I feel like that neutrality affected [our] third album."

For album four, of course, the direction was shamelessly commercial, radio-friendly, danceable pop tracks. In a wry nod to the fact that such a deliberately mainstream album was clearly timed to coincide with the second series of *The Voice*, the group had already decided what to call it: *Overexposed*.

"In order to avoid being accused of overexposure or of overexposing ourselves, we needed to nip it in the bud," Adam claimed. "Say it before everyone else did." He added triumphantly: "You can't get sick of us if we're already sick of ourselves."

However, one Maroon 5 member was already a little sick of the overexposure and was bowing out quietly. Jesse's current aim was to focus on both his solo music project, 1863, and the healing arts – which for him encompassed spirituality, meditation, psychic intuition and energy and faith healing – before returning to the group in time for the fifth album.

Watching Adam evolve as an individual outside of the band had reminded Jesse of his own personal interests, which he had long since neglected. By necessity of the near-endless touring schedule to which life in an internationally famous band had committed him, Jesse the individual had all but disappeared. His hiatus would be a temporary one, giving him the chance to regain an identity outside of Maroon 5 before coming back, refreshed and with renewed dedication.

Allowing PJ Morton to step up his duties and take over Jesse's role, the group returned fulltime to the studio. One of the earliest songs that emerged was 'Ladykiller', which bore similarities to the sonic style of Adam's favourite childhood band, Hall & Oates. The lyrics were teasingly ambiguous and intentionally thought-provoking: they clearly referred to an unfaithful lover, but was the other person who'd captured the heart of Adam's girlfriend male or female? The lyric suggested the latter, adding a little intrigue to the love triangle, but either way, he was begging for his unfaithful partner to come back to his side.

'Love Somebody' depicted a game of seduction on the dance floor, while the funk and dubstep-infused 'Lucky Strike', which spoke of shaking like an earthquake as a metaphor for orgasm, detailed the sex that would be the end result. 'Doin' Dirt' was an electro-pop track with a shamelessly open lyric about an illicit affair between two partners who are already attached elsewhere, making reference to exhibitionistic public sex and hinting at S&M.

'Tickets' was another track with an ambiguous meaning – Adam talks of someone who relies purely on family connections rather than talent or hard work to carry them through life, who has had an easy ride they might not have deserved. If, as with several other newer Maroon 5 songs, the skeleton of the track had been written years earlier, then it might have been assumed to be a dig at Adam's ex-girlfriend, Jane. However, it seems more likely it was aimed at the often incestuous nature of celebrity, using the female character as a metaphor for Adam's contempt for the culture of fame. He speaks of someone perfect on the outside but empty at the core – perhaps a reference to the superficiality of celebrity culture, where looks often count for more than talent, style is an accepted substitute for substance and fluffy vacuity regularly takes the place of real-life issues.

Despite knowing that the person he craves is vacuous, Adam admits that he gives in to temptation and, instead of resisting, will do his best to "get you off". Behind this lyric of sexual encounter, could it be the story of how, in spite of initial scepticism, Adam was persuaded to join the world of reality TV? As some perceived him as selling out and joining the celebrity circus he'd always spoken out against, perhaps in his own way he was using 'Tickets' to reiterate his contempt for fame for its own sake and to distance his own career trajectory from those associations.

It was troubling for Adam that some saw his spiralling success as a bad thing – although, for the most part, he felt audiences appreciated the difference between *The Voice*, which he insisted was "built on positivity", and rivals such as *American Idol*. He also felt grateful that the majority of his fans appeared not to judge him for his embrace of TV culture.

"I think that there was this generation before us that was so hellbent on not selling out that it went too far," he asserted, "and I feel like maybe history is correcting itself because it's more acceptable now to do a lot of things that musicians would have been terrified to do 10 years ago. I was never that guy that thought it was uncool for a band to be successful. I always thought, 'Wow, wouldn't it be amazing to be able to pay your bills and also be a musician?'"

Yet there was still a side of him that would always feel torn – an ambivalence that had seen the switch to reality TV not as a comfortable choice but as a lifeline, after his career as a serious musician had begun to dwindle. Perhaps it was that dilemma to which he referred when, at the start of the track, he sang of a concert no one wanted to attend.

There was a return to the relationship theme with 'The Man Who Never Lied', depicting a dramatic argument in the middle of Hollywood Boulevard which culminates in an uneasy lie, to save him from breaking his lover's heart. Meanwhile 'Fortune Teller' may perhaps have related to the rising tension between Adam and Anne V; no one knew it at the time, particularly as that summer had seen the pair posing naked together for an erotic photo shoot to grace the front cover of Russian *Vogue*, but their relationship was fraught with disagreements. Anne had been looking for answers as to where their relationship was heading and, according to popular rumour, had been pressuring him to consider marriage.

It was a thorny subject for Adam – having experienced the trauma of his parents' divorce, aged seven, and having seen the statistics that confirmed their situation was not the exception but the norm, he was loath to rush into anything hastily. In fact, he would clarify to *Paper* magazine that, while he was "extremely fascinated" by the concept of marriage, he was adamant that, "I'm not just going to rush into it, because that's not good for anybody."

Those words were not music to Anne's ears, however, and in 'Fortune Teller', he seemed to lyrically accuse her of ruining yet another night by asking him to predict the future. Wearily and at times almost scornfully, he asserts that he is far from a fortune teller himself, adding that her American Dream – perhaps involving the traditional fantasy of marriage and two children – is just not for him. He wants simply to enjoy the moment, while she wants to meticulously plan the next one. She wants to commit, while he wants to take things slowly and live for today. It was a fundamental incompatibility that, in the heat of their relationship, neither wanted to admit to – and one that would ultimately lead to their break-up.

Yet it might not be a permanent situation. 'One More Night' depicts an ill-fated couple who feel enormous passion between them but are badly suited, leaving a withdrawing Adam to feel "guilty as hell" for repeatedly giving in to temptation with her. Their love has become an unsolvable conundrum – the reasons they were attracted to one another in the first place still remain, but equally they split up for a reason and their relationship stands no chance of lasting.

The final bittersweet night together, before summoning the willpower to break away for good, is depicted in 'Daylight', which sees Adam dreading the morning as it means facing the last goodbye. 'Beautiful Goodbye', as its title suggests, features a similar dilemma.

'Sad' captures the yearning for the relationship to continue and the uncertainty of whether he chose the right path when he left it behind. Finally, 'Payphone', written a year earlier and featuring a verse by the rapper Wiz Khalifa, saw the ending of a relationship move into a new phase: bitterness. Plans made for two are cruelly cut in half, fairytales are described as "full of shit" and love songs are virtually vomit-inducing.

Then the group added three bonus tracks: 'Wasted Years' was a revitalised song that dated back to the *Songs About Jane* era, featuring the same theme of a passionate relationship turned sour – a predicament that had since become all too common in Adam's life. 'Wipe Your Eyes', meanwhile, was a sentimental ballad involving repentantly comforting a lover whose heart he had broken.

Finally, the group had made the audacious decision to cover Prince's 'Kiss' – something which met with barely disguised disapproval from the performer himself. "Why do we need to hear another cover of a song someone else did?" questioned the artist known as Prince. "Art is about building a new foundation, not just laying something on top of what's already there."

As the band placed the finishing touches on *Overexposed* – the fastest album they'd ever recorded – they paused to attend the 2012 Grammys. However, Adam would announce that they'd changed the location of their post-ceremony celebrations after learning that the owners of the (unnamed) Mexican-themed restaurant they'd formerly attended annually had provided financial backing for Proposition 8. While they didn't name the homophobic eatery that supported the withdrawal of rights for gay couples, they broke their tradition of dining there on Grammys night – and their custom was no doubt sorely missed.

February 2012 would also see the launch of Adam's independent record label, 222 – the project he'd longed for had finally come to fruition. By taking the reins of the label, not only were he and other band members guaranteed total creative control over their fifth album, but he was also able to provide a launch pad for up and coming artists he believed in.

His first signing was actor Matthew Morrison, best known for his role in the TV series *Glee*. His self-titled album had made it to number 24 on the

US *Billboard* chart and, for his follow-up, he'd switched from the well-known Mercury Records to 222, despite its status as a newcomer.

Adam was now not just a judge, mentor and musician, but also a talent scout – and when he returned to his chair for the second series of *The Voice*, he had his eye trained on promising contestant Tony Lucca. Tony had quickly been signed to Adam's team and caused the first fight of the series, between his coach and a furious Christina Aguilera.

Adam's appetite for rock and hip-hop fusion, blending different sounds in seeming opposition into the same song, was the standout trait that had seen Maroon 5 signed to a record label, and he encouraged Tony to take on the same style with a rock version of Jay-Z's '99 Problems'. Unfortunately, Christina took issue with the colourful language of the song. Jay-Z, who labelled himself a 'pimp' on tracks and was often accused of making sexism a selling point, had rapped that, while he had 99 problems, a 'bitch' wasn't one of them.

Although the expletive was edited out before the show aired, it didn't escape Christina's ears. "Your beautiful wife and your daughter and your family are here tonight," she reminded Tony sternly. "I just thought the lyrical connotation was a little derogatory towards women."

It seemed an unusual stance for Christina to take as her own songs had described her as a "super-bitch", yet the point she was making was clear. Adam hit back, defending the song and claiming it was about a struggle with adversity. It sparked a heated exchange. Christina, who had starred alongside Tony in *The New Mickey Mouse Club* in her preteen years, allegedly continued the altercation backstage; according to the rumour mill of the time, this supposedly led to Adam branding her "the biggest fucking cunt" and her hissing back that he ought to be fired. Quotes attributed to Christina claimed, "If America knew how disgusting he was, they would be appalled."

In actual fact, Adam had previously admitted to "bickering" with Christina but claimed to have given it up when he realised he couldn't deliver his blows with the "charm" of his co-star, Blake Shelton. Certainly, labelling someone a "fucking cunt" was about as far from gentle, witty repartee as it was possible to get, but Adam soon rubbished the reports of in-fighting as "fictional", adding that the media rumours had been fundamentally untrue: "We never hated each other [and] never had these secret battles that everyone thought we were having."

In spite of the controversial Jay-Z lyrics, Adam would stand up for women's rights in a subsequent episode when he refused to pick a contestant on the basis that the hopeful chose to cover a track by Chris Brown. Following the vocalist's infamous 2009 attack on his then girlfriend, Rihanna, leaving her face bruised and covered in blood, Adam had expressed open contempt for Brown.

As for Tony Lucca, Adam was almost relieved when his protégé failed to win *The Voice* and its accompanying record contract, as it gave him carte blanche to sign him to 222 Records, whereupon he would take an active role in planning his debut as a recording artist.

Meanwhile, on a personal level the overexposure was just beginning. In April, just as *The Voice's* second series was in full swing, the single 'Payphone' hit the charts – and Maroon 5 performed it for the first time live on the show. Within hours of its April 17, 2012 release, the song exploded. It sold 493,000 digital copies in the first week, providing the best sales week of all time for a digital song by a group. It wasn't merely due to their stateside overexposure on *The Voice* either – the single topped the charts in the UK for the first time in the group's history and it also hit the top spot in Canada. Overall, it would become the fifth bestselling single of 2012, with over nine million copies sold.

As the success of the single broke worldwide records, it was announced that Adam would also try his hand at acting, with a guest role in the heart-pounding TV series *American Horror Story*. His character, a newly-wed photographer, would take his wife on an unconventional honeymoon, touring as many haunted locations as possible before deciding to get sexual at their final stop – the less than romantic former mental asylum Briarcliff Manor. As it turned out, the horror element was the least of his worries.

"The first thing I did when I got the job," a slightly nervous Adam would confess, "was ask friends who are actors what the fuck I was supposed to do."

To make matters worse, he admitted his lack of interest in the series to one of its creators, Ryan Murphy. "I don't like the horror genre much," he would explain with disarming candour, "so I told Ryan. I basically said, 'I don't like this show.'" He also admitted that he feared exposing his ineptitude as an actor, adding, "I told him I really didn't know what I was doing, but he didn't seem to really care!"

However, if all else failed, there was a chance for him to capitalise on his sex appeal. Since appearing in Russian *Vogue* in the altogether and doing a smaller solo shoot for *Cosmopolitan* to raise awareness for testicular cancer – in which a beaming yet slightly sheepish Adam's modesty had been covered by a strategically placed female hand – he'd topped numerous 'Sexiest Male' lists.

From topping *Glamour* magazine's 'Sexiest Men Of 2011' poll to receiving an honourable mention in *Shalom Life* declaring him one of the most gorgeous Jewish men in the world, it seemed as though his abs had taken on a celebrity profile of their own – and they'd be making a guest appearance when filming for *American Horror Story*. However, if he'd thought he'd need to rely on sex appeal to disguise a lack of acting ability, he needn't have worried – Murphy was convinced he was the new Justin Timberlake.

While he plucked up the courage to enter acting territory, the video for 'Payphone' – which debuted on May 10 – provided him with some practice. Dubbed a mini-movie by critics, it saw him play the hero at a Las Vegas bank by snatching a gun from a group of robbers – some played by his bandmates – and thwarting their heist, before going on the run after being mistaken by police for one of the villains. Stepping into a custom 1967 Shelby Cobra car – which Adam had built himself from a kit during a break from touring – he flees, cradling a shot arm in the process. During the car chase, one of the police vehicles bursts into flames and, eventually, Adam's own ride does the same.

Disheartened and deflated, he turns to a payphone to pour out his tortured love song, begging his other half not to hang up. Adam viewed using a phone box as the ultimate metaphor for needing help: with mobile phones so ubiquitous and tariffs so inexpensive, he felt only a truly desperate situation would call for resorting to a payphone.

Yet unusually, as sharp eyes may have spotted, his partner in crime for the video was not Anne V but a rival Victoria's Secret model, Bregje Heinen – and news reports would soon reveal exactly why.

Adam's parallel singing/talent show/acting career was at an all-time high, yet his success would be blighted by a break-up with Anne – one which was so sudden that, by his own account, it left him "blindsided".

She had released an official statement confirming the couple's separation but, according to rumour, she'd neglected to tell Adam first, who'd merely thought their relationship was troubled and hanging in the balance until further discussion.

It was widely speculated upon that Anne had been ready for marriage, but that – as 'Fortune Teller' had predicted – Adam had been reluctant to make that kind of promise. Anne had also felt that living with a platonic male friend in his thirties as Adam did was inappropriate, akin to a student sharing a dorm. Regardless of what she said, however, he refused to be pinned down and his biggest concession to domesticity was framing a nude photo from one of Anne's modelling shoots and placing it on his bedside table. The couple were incompatible but, blinded by sexual attraction, they refused to see it.

Before Adam could process his loss, it was time to move on. It was ironic that the next single, 'One More Night', released on June 19, dealt with a similar scenario. The video opened with an image of two goldfish swimming aimlessly around a bowl – a metaphor for the vicious circle of desperately wanting to leave an unsuitable relationship but continually being tempted back in, trapped by an addiction to a lover. The plot centres on Adam as a boxer, fighting to support his wife and young daughter. However, trouble is continually brewing and, after winning one major fight, he returns home to an empty house, having lost his family for good. The reggae rhythms of the track won the group its most successful stateside single yet – it would claim the number one spot on the *Billboard* chart for nine consecutive weeks.

June also saw Adam net a second acting opportunity, starring opposite Keira Knightley in *Can A Song Save Your Life?* The pair played aspiring musicians in love who move to New York to pursue fame. Yet flighty Adam soon breaks up with Keira to become a solo celebrity – which is when the adventure for both parties really begins.

Although Adam was telling anyone who would listen that he was a hopeless actor who'd stumbled into the job by accident, knew little of what to do and was almost doomed to fail, his manager, Jordan Feldstein, begged to differ, insisting, "It's a personal passion . . . something that he's legitimately been talking to me about for 15 years."

Whatever the truth, it was clear that – unlike the first time around – his confidence as an actor was building. In fact he now regarded it a simpler task than his 'day job'.

"You get onstage and perform in front of 10,000 people and if you fuck up, it's your ass," he reflected. "[On the other hand] how scary is it to go into an intimate setting that's totally comfortable and do something 500 times until you get it right? That's not pressure."

That was evident from Adam's demeanour on set – he wore casual checked shirts and geeky glasses, while laughing and joking animatedly with Keira, seemingly oblivious to the cameras. For him, this project was a break from the fast-paced, adrenalin-fuelled atmosphere of the tour – almost a respite.

Meanwhile Jesse – who'd been off the touring circuit for considerably longer – released his debut solo EP of experimental music, entitled simply *Five Songs*. It was made available as a digital download, as encouraged by his bandmates.

Soon after, Maroon 5 returned to the grindstone. Following Adam's hostility towards MTV for its alleged lack of interest in music – which culminated in a furious tweet reading "Fuck the VMAs!" – the group were astonished to find they'd still been nominated for an award at the very same ceremony in honour of 'Payphone', losing out only to One Direction's 'What Makes You Beautiful'.

Soon after, Adam's first episode of *American Horror Story* would air on TV. The preview clip posted on Facebook would boast, "Only we can make insanity this sexy" – and the episode included a bare-chested Adam writhing around with his scantily clad co-star on a hospital bed complete with straps for restraint. Unfortunately, the pair would find themselves with unexpected company – and subsequent scenes saw Adam gagged with a blood-spattered T-shirt, attempting unsuccessfully to ward off a masked serial killer and finally losing his arm as it gets brutally ripped from its socket by a monstrous unseen presence.

It was all so gory that a petrified Adam struggled even to play back his scenes to critique his own acting. "When I watched back a little bit of it, I was terrified of everything!" he exclaimed, before adding, "I might as well never watch that show again. What the hell was that? That show is totally fucked up. It was really hard to watch, because it's just so weird and disturbing."

Fortunately his gory screen debut wasn't a deterrent for new partner Behati Prinsloo – yet another Victoria's Secret model, this time hailing from Namibia. Behati was a regular in fashion magazines, having graced the cover of *Vogue* in the USA and Russia, and *Elle* in France, Sweden and Italy. She was also a catwalk star for brands such as Chanel, Miu Miu and Prada, her fame even exceeding that of Adam's previous partner.

By now, Adam had started to become the butt of incredulous jokes for repeatedly romancing models. That status earned him the tag of 'modellist', a term jokingly coined by Carrie Bradshaw of *Sex & The City* to refer to a man who exclusively dates catwalk girls.

Yet it was the ultimate cliché for a high profile musician to date a model and, with his pay on *The Voice* increasing to $6 million per season in time for the third series, he certainly fitted that description. He and Behati, who had secretly been seeing each other for months, soon began 'officially' dating, making their first public appearance together at the *GQ* Gentlemen's Ball in October.

The following month, as third single 'Daylight' hit the charts, Adam found himself at the mercy of another bout of verbal diarrhoea – perfect for playful banter on *The Voice*, but a little more controversial when applied to events outside the TV studio. After a contestant performed a Michelle Branch song, Adam had a flashback to his lowly past when he hadn't been able to score so much as a dressing room, let alone a top model.

"We used to open for Michelle Branch," he raged on at the confused hopeful, "and I remember we opened for her at the Roxy and they didn't even give us a dressing room. I hate the Roxy. I'll never play there again."

Perhaps unintentionally delivering some lucrative publicity for the venue – after all, his comments were made on a primetime national TV show – he continued. "The Roxy's horrible. Don't ever go there. They screwed us over and now they're paying for it."

. The Sunset Strip nightclub, defending that it was "at the mercy of the headliner" when it came to allocating rooms, responded with a huge sign outside that quipped: "Adam Levine, your dressing room is ready!"

Next Adam turned his attention to spoilt seven-year-old pageant queen Alana 'Honey Boo Boo' Thompson, whose series, *Here Comes Honey Boo Boo*, was a hit on US TV. She'd been praised for her tolerance when, despite hailing from a devoutly religious rural town in the Deep South, she'd remarked charitably of her uncle's sexuality, "Ain't nothing wrong with being a little gay!" However, others frowned upon the cocktail of caffeine-fuelled energy drinks her mother fed her to prepare for pageants. They highlighted possible exploitation by her family, who earned a reported $50,000 for each episode of the show, and also questioned the wisdom of reinforcing the message that looks are all-important and a more valuable commodity than achievements or intelligence. To critics, this implied stance presented a young and impressionable girl with a warped view of the world. They felt the emphasis on her appearance as a measure of self-worth might cause eating disorders, low self-esteem, and even plastic surgery addiction in later life, as she desperately strived to maintain popularity in a fickle, superficial media world she was not yet mature enough to handle. Did the show send the message that perfection was not just coveted but expected of her – that she could only be loved if she was beautiful? Adam certainly thought so.

In fact, he was one of the show's fiercest critics, arguing, "Seriously, *Here Comes Honey Boo Boo* is the DECAY of Western civilisation. Just because so many people watch it doesn't mean it's good. So many people witness atrocities and can't take their eyes away from them, but that doesn't mean they're good. That show is literally The. Worst. Thing. That's. Ever. Happened. It's complete fucking ignorance and the most despicable way to treat your kids. Fuck those people. You can put that in the magazine. Fuck those idiots. They're just the worst. Sorry, I'm so sensitive to that – like, I don't know, man, it's upsetting." In case the message hadn't yet got through, he added, "Just to clarify, I said FUCK THOSE PEOPLE!"

Adam was by now gaining a near unrivalled reputation in showbiz for outspokenness, but one of his widely publicised comments would come back to haunt him when he committed what he'd previously claimed was the biggest possible *faux pas* in celebrity land: launching a fragrance. By February 2013, when the news emerged that he would be teaming up with ID Perfumes to create his own signature scent, co-judge Christina Aguilera was quick to tease that he was a hypocrite. Unearthing a former Twitter post from Adam's archives which read, "I would like to put an official ban on celebrity fragrances. Punishable by death from this point forward," she jibed, "Haha @AdamLevine. What a difference a year makes!"

Most would be cringeing with embarrassment, but an unrepentant and unfazed Adam – when questioned on his 'punishable by death' policy, would merely retort, "Yes and I will die some day." He added: "Of course I hate celebrity fragrances. They're lame – but I was given the opportunity and I thought, 'Well, I think that I've got decent taste and will be able to do it in a way that's not offensive . . . and they are paying me, so that's part of it.'"

While others might have dubbed him a hypocrite – and not unreasonably – his frank honesty, without a hint of regard for media gloss or pre-rehearsed PR spiel, was exactly why Adam had grown so popular. In a world of increasingly fake showbiz sentiment aimed purely at promoting and preserving one's own public image, he had refused to be driven by fear of public opinion. Even if his statements were offensive, controversial and self-deprecating, it seemed he could always be relied upon to tell the truth.

The fragrance, which would appear in Macy's department stores and feature its own microphone-shaped bottle, was truly a signature scent – and not merely by name alone. Proving that he had very definite ideas of the product that would bear his logo, he told *Us Weekly*: "Because I don't really enjoy wearing cologne, I want to create a kind of anti-cologne, something you could wear as an alternative or as an answer to a lot of the things that are out there."

Adamant that the men's fragrance had to be "simple and citric . . . refreshing instead of musky", he added, "I like it to be something you don't smell a mile away. Same with the women's. With the women's, it's something you can enjoy if you're in close proximity to a woman and smell her neck or her arm or something – I don't like being bombarded by a whole flower garden or marshmallows." To him, his input was significant because, in his own eyes, "If you're going to get paid to do this ridiculous shit, you've got to put fucking effort into it."

Adam took another step towards shameless overexposure in February 2013, when he announced that he would be teaming up with Sears to design clothes and accessories for both genders under a new lifestyle brand. As Sears owned brands such as K-Mart, it was destined to go mainstream.

However, in that same month, when he performed a mash-up with

Alicia Keys at the 2013 Grammys, comprising 'Daylight' and a version of her new track 'Girl On Fire', he was bringing it firmly back to the music – an indicator that, no matter how lucrative the business deals became, this was where his heart truly lay.

It seemed comical that he didn't even attempt to disguise his contempt for the world of celebrity fragrances – one he openly branded ridiculous – even after he'd signed up to create one. That he was heavily involved with numerous corporate deals and yet unafraid to blast the same corporations in the name of free speech was a signature of his uncompromising stance – a trademark which he brought to the creation of his own record label.

While the stereotypes about Adam had been abundant over the years, branding him a superficial 'modelliser' (or 'modellist') who was more interested in women than music, his passionate interest in politics and culture, as well as his presentation of himself as a serious musician, had forced critics to rethink their attitudes. His openness had brought Adam closer to sharing the 'real him' – and the other members of Maroon 5, similarly intrigued by politics and spirituality, had also begun to step out of the shadows.

Yet the ultimate test is due in the form of Maroon 5's fifth album, currently under construction and due for release on 222 in 2014. The self-publishing format will offer Adam and his bandmates – including the newly returned Jesse – total creative control. No longer tied by the protocol of a corporate regime, when it comes to deciphering who the band really are beneath the media sheen, the next album should stand as their most illuminating yet.

The future's bright – the future's maroon.